A RESTORATION STORY

JENNY THOMPSON

WESTBOW
PRESS®
A DIVISION OF THOMAS NELSON
& ZONDERVAN

WestBow Press books may be ordered through booksellers or by contacting:

WestBow Press
A Division of Thomas Nelson & Zondervan
1663 Liberty Drive
Bloomington, IN 47403
www.westbowpress.com
844-714-3454

ISBN: 979-8-3850-2889-4 (sc)
ISBN: 979-8-3850-2890-0 (e)

Library of Congress Control Number: 2024914289

Print information available on the last page.

WestBow Press rev. date: 07/20/2024

CONTENTS

chapter

1

INTRODUCTION

September 5, 2013

"I am so sorry. Please, pray and give me privacy." -Facebook

I did not want to remember. I have been keeping journals since I was eleven years old. Why would I document any of this? I was entering the darkest season of my life, and I felt the Holy Spirit stirring in me to write. What would I write? How hurt I was, how embarrassed I was, and how confused I was? Sure, that would be in there. But God wanted me to write more. Strategy. Honesty. Transparency. A journal of a waiting woman. But waiting for what? Restoration. Healing.

I remember thinking that the process of restoration would take less than a year. I even had a scripture for it. Jeremiah 17:8 (NIV) says, "They will be like a tree planted by the water that sends out its roots by the stream. It does not fear when heat comes; its leaves are always green. It has no worries in A YEAR of drought and never fails to bear fruit." I believe in the truth of God's Word, and I latched on to this verse as pertaining to my situation. It had to be for me, right? I could do this for

1

a year. Little did I know that start to finish would be a lot longer than that. It would not be an easy, cut and dried process.

The truth of God's word did not fail me. I used scripture to try to dictate God's will and timing. It doesn't work like that, folks! God had a perfect plan for my story. Satan tempted Jesus in the wilderness by using scripture. He knows scripture. I remember the year coming to an end and I felt such disappointment. It cast a shadow of doubt that the enemy would try to use over the remainder of my journey to restoration.

Everyone supported me in my journey. Sadly, this is not true. There were those that would stand in faith with me, but they felt like few. The majority, especially as time waned, would wish me to move on. There are many reasons for this, and now I understand more. I'm not angry at them. People didn't want to see me hurting anymore. People didn't believe that Cal deserved me. People were angry at my husband. I had "biblical reason" to move on. People couldn't see themselves fighting the way that I was, and there may have been some guilt in that thought process. I heard so many reasons to let him go. But God said no.

It was difficult to start my journey journal. A vocal professor from college told my voice class to write things down to help with the memorization process. That is fine and dandy for memorizing a song, but this was different. I didn't start my journal right away. I still needed a little convincing from the Lord.

I am a private person, but I was living a very public life. People were asking my family questions, and I knew that I had to have some transparency online. People will draw their own conclusions otherwise. Rumor mills flourish in dark places. I wanted people to pray.

I made some rules for myself. I would not bad mouth my husband and I would be discreet in my details. I would not pretend like everything was ok when it was not. I wanted to show faith but be honest when I needed help in my faith. I wanted to be encouraged and I wanted to encourage others. I wanted a Testimony.

2

A LOVE STORY AND A
TRAIN WRECK

The year was 1992. I was a senior in high school. My family and I had recently moved to Ukiah, California to pastor a church. Ukiah was such a pretty town, nestled in the wine country. There was a vineyard walking distance from my house. Tollini Lane was lovely. The row of houses on both sides of the street led down to Calvary Way Pentecostal Church of God. The parsonage was on the church property. I had never lived on church property before, and I loved it. I could walk next door and play the piano any time I wanted.

I am a pianist and singer.

I remember so clearly the Sunday that Calvin drove onto the church property. He was on a black motorcycle, complete with a black leather jacket and a lime green sweater poking out underneath. He had blond hair with a hint of curls in the back from letting it grow out. "How much will you give me for his phone number?'" asked a man named Tim who caught me gawking. "I'll get it myself," I replied. I was inexperienced, so I honestly had no idea how to achieve this feat.

We had a testimony service that morning. Cal stood up and said, "God delivered me from drugs, alcohol and women." My mother leaned over to me and said, "Stay away from that one'" Calvin was twenty-two years of age, and I was seventeen. Calvin was experienced, and I was naïve. I did not care.

Calvin began attending our church regularly. I turned eighteen, and Cal invited me to a Bible study four days later. I drove to the Bible study, not sure if this was a "date" or not. It didn't matter. I was going to spend time with him. When the Bible study was over, he invited me over to his house where a group of friends planned to watch a concert video. When I arrived at his cute, little one bedroom house on Talmage Road, which he shared with a roommate, he jumped in the car with me. His friends arrived and we stayed in the car. We talked and never went inside.

We talked about life and relationships. I was not sure if he was interested in me, so I just asked him directly, "is there someone you're interested in?" He looked at me incredulously and proclaimed, "You!" I was so happy! He went on to tell me, however, that he would not kiss until his wedding day. Kissing led to other things, and he did not want that temptation in his life. I was not happy about that, to say the least. Kissing was all virgins like me had to look forward to! I did not understand his struggle. I did not understand his past. I did not understand what he was trying to be free from. I wish I had.

The next few months, I worked for that kiss! I finally got it. Thinking about it now, I feel guilty. I was innocent. I would spend many years unaware of my husband's struggles. A Godly woman is a helpmeet to her husband, Was I? I was not in this arena.

We were married fifteen months later, on July 10, 1993. I was the Worship Director at Calvary Way, and I taught piano and voice lessons. Calvin worked at a rental store and served as the Junior Church Director. We grew up together as ministers in the church. We served as Junior leaders, youth pastors, assistant pastors and then head pastors.

Over the next twenty years, we built a beautiful family. Caleb was born in 1994, Ramona arrived in 1996, and Lonnie came in 1999. We suffered a miscarriage in 2005. I have a sweet little one in Heaven (what a place to grow up!). God blessed us with Callie in 2006. I am so thankful for our children.

My parents became the Northern California/Nevada Bishops for the Pentecostal Church of God in 2007. Calvary Way Church voted Calvin and I in as the head pastors. I loved my church, and I loved my town. We were successful.

Our church grew in number. We pastored for six years. The last year of our tenure was the worst. The church seemed successful by outside appearances, but it was crumbling within. I thought my husband was having a nervous breakdown. Life was busy. Cal was losing weight. We began arguing more, mostly about doctrine. He would still preach sound doctrine from the pulpit, but at home, he was speaking thoughts that frightened me. I was nervous every time he would preach. I did not understand what was happening to my husband.

"Is Cal on drugs?" a church member asked me. "No!" I exclaimed. How could anyone think that? It had to be a nervous breakdown. Wouldn't a wife know if her husband was using drugs? I saw him every day. Surely, I would know. His erratic behavior was spilling into the community. People were not blind. People were not deaf. I was in denial. It had to be something as simple as, "he needs to rest and clear his head."

Cal said that he was offered an opportunity to go to a church in Oregon for a week. A Sabbatical was what he needed. The Church Board agreed, and I agreed. I found out later that it was not a church, and it was by no means a Holy Sabbatical. The train was barreling down the track that was our lives together, and there was about to be a terrible collision.

The phone call came while I was putting away laundry. I was in my son's bedroom. I answered, happy to hear from my husband. He did not sound well. He proceeded to confess his sins to me. He had another life. He had fought addiction to pornography during our entire marriage. He was having affairs, drinking, and using drugs. I stood there, silent. "Are you there?" he asked. "I'm listening." I replied. I was in shock. He confessed his sins and wanted to make things right.

To be completely honest in my writings, I must admit that he told me of his addiction to pornography a few years before. I didn't handle it well. "I'm a pornographic fiend." I remember those words so clearly, scarred into my brain. We were driving in a car, on a date. He had dealt with pornography from a young age. He was getting help. He needed to confess to me to "get it into the light." He had an accountability partner. He was reading a book. He was getting help. I didn't want to be "that wife" that needed all the passwords, watched over his shoulder, or worried about it. I could not handle it. I buried it. I failed my husband.

I was torn. There was no burying this. There was no drowning truth in the sea of denial. My parents were my District pastors. I needed to tell them. I needed help, but what was I to say? I wanted to stay at my church but knew that we needed to resign. I did not want to. I had been at Calvary Way Church since I was the age of seventeen! My friends were there. Calvary Way was part of my family heritage. My kids were in school. My kids! How would I tell them? I was numb. I wanted to do right by my husband, by my church, by my family and by my denominational church. I wanted to do what was right in the eyes of my God!

I did not have to decide. Calvin did it for me. Once he confessed, he felt like he was free. Everything was in the light. He went off the rails. Things crumbled so quickly.

He used profanity on Facebook. People noticed. It was not the Cal that any of us knew. My parents saw. I was mortified. I was so angry at him. I was embarrassed. I responded to the situation on Facebook.

September 5, 2013

"I am so sorry. Please pray and give me privacy."

September 6, 2013

"Although we are in a rough season, our leaves are still green, and we have been bearing fruit. I hope people will stick by us and give us a chance to stay in the place we love. So many people are talking about my family right now-good and bad. We love Calvary Way Church very much. We have never claimed to be perfect people, and any pastor who says they are, are mistaken or lying. I hope to receive some of the grace that we've been teaching for so long."

I see now that I was grasping at straws. A tearing down had to happen for true deliverance and restoration to happen.

My parents arranged to be at our church that Sunday to address the issue. Church began as normal. I led worship. Calvin and I then stood before a packed house. Calvin addressed the church and then he addressed my parents. He looked at me, looked at them and said, "you want her, you got her." He walked off the platform and out the door. I did not chase after him. This was the Lord's Day, and I had a job to do. Calvin was in God's hands. He had a Savior, and I was not Him. I told the church people that the service would continue as planned. I do not know how I did it. Well, I do. Only God. I sang a special song, and my dad preached the Word of God. I do not remember anything else about that day. My mom told me recently how a group of us talked around the piano after the service. I remember absolutely nothing.

What would come next? This was uncharted territory for me.

SEPTEMBER 12, 2013- Facebook

"When I think of all I have to do in the next couple months and wondering what lies ahead, I get a little overwhelmed. BUT I keep my eyes focused on Jesus and listen for the strategy He has for me to accomplish it all. If He gives you the strategy, you know it won't fail! I'm listening, Jesus"

I stayed in the parsonage for three months. It was so important to me to close that chapter of my life with dignity. My grandparents had pastored Calvary Way. My parents had pastored Calvary Way. My husband and I pastored Calvary Way. I didn't want to leave that precious place in ruin. So, I preached. I led worship. I dedicated a baby to the Lord. I taught music. I made sure that all the church financial books were in order and properly closed. I packed up my house. I tried to find a house to rent in the area, but every door closed in my face. I would need to take my kids to Sacramento, to live with my parents. I was thirty-nine years old, moving back in with my parents. I was losing everything.

My parents were amazing. I was welcomed and encouraged to come to Sacramento. When I posted my feelings online (written above), both of my parents responded in true fashion. This is who they are.

Dad-

"Psalm 61:1-4 NKJV Hear my cry, O God; Attend to my prayer. From the end of the earth, I will cry to You, when my heart is overwhelmed; Lead me to the rock that is higher than I. For You have been a shelter for me, a strong tower from the enemy. I will abide in Your tabernacle forever; I will trust in the shelter of Your wings. Selah."

Mom-

"Your dad always has the exact scripture needed for the appointed time. As your mom, just let me know when you need my help hiding the body! Lol"

The three months following our resignation were tough with Calvin. He was unchained. In his mind, he was free to be himself finally. He didn't have to fight anymore. He had been fighting for so long. He had spent years of crying in the altars. He had spent years trying to do what was right. The addictions always came calling. Sometimes he would answer, and sometimes he would not. He would make it long periods of time without a slip. I have never doubted that he loved Jesus during these times. There was a root that needed to be dug up and burned to be truly free.

From my perspective, where the fight changed was when he thought it did not affect his salvation. He was just as saved as the rest of us. I remember his offense at the idea that we saw him as lost. He was not lost, he was "free." We were the problem, not him. The Pentecostal Church of God was the problem, not him. I was the problem, not him. In his mind, which was voiced to me many times over our ordeal, I was the one who had him in bondage all those years. He would come to hate me for it. The truth is that he had so much freedom, he hung himself with it. In his mind, I held the rope.

He would disappear on the weekends. I would not know where he was. He would come home for a few days to sleep off whatever damage he had done to himself that weekend. Strange things were happening in my home. Things became very dark.

Calvin would leave food out for the creatures who lived in the trees, I remember him telling me about something being in one of the trees by the Sanctuary. I told him there was nothing there. I wanted to convince him, so I marched over to that tree. I was praying desperately, "God, please don't let there be anything in that tree!" There was nothing. Well, there was nothing that I could see.

One night, I woke to find Cal standing over me. It was so scary. I closed my eyes and prayed. He walked away. There was another night when Callie woke us up screaming because of the shape of a man she saw standing over our bed. Her dad told her that it was an Angel. It was not the good kind. Good kinds do not produce that kind of terror. Later, I saw the same spirit. I was standing in the bathroom getting ready for the day. I saw a full figure, shadow of a man walking by the front door. Calvin was not home at the time.

I asked God to show me the drugs. I remember a clear picture in my mind telling me where they were. I climbed in the driver's seat of my car, reached back and felt beneath the passenger seat. I pulled out a bank bag. Inside was an empty plastic bag with residue, needles, and a spoon. The spoon had burn marks on it. I took the bag and its contents and put them in the church dumpster. Cal was very angry with me. "There's a proper way to dispose of it!" I wouldn't tell him where I put it, just that it was long gone.

There was a time when flies covered the ceiling of our living room. There wasn't a place you could touch where there was not a fly. It was like a scene out of a horror movie. Calvin thought it was from the winery down the street. No such thing had happened in that home before. Why now? My home was not just my home anymore. Jesus covered me and our children. He protected us. Worlds were colliding. It was like a Peretti novel. I am glad that my eyes were not fully opened to the spiritual battle that was happening on that property. I would probably be in a psych hospital.

December came and it was time to go. I would not let people help me clean. I wouldn't let people help me move a lifetime of things into a storage unit. I was embarrassed and I felt stronger alone. I had to leave the piano that I first learned to play on, in the house. It was an antique. I don't know what happened to it. I don't want to know. The day that we left, Cal was nowhere in sight. I loaded up our Trailblazer with our four kids, three dogs, one cat and one goldfish and headed to Sacramento with nothing but the clothes on our backs and a few suitcases. I remember physically feeling the weight (the pastoral burden) of the church lifting from my shoulders. I did not realize how heavy it was until it was gone

December 11, 2013

"Goodbye Ukiah." "I made it to Sac."

I remember walking into my parents' house, which was now my house, and plopping down on the sofa. I was numb. I had no job, no home of my own, no ministry and no husband. My plate felt empty.

God ordered my steps. I would teach music full-time and I would join the Worship team at my brother's church, playing the piano and singing back-up vocals. I had a hard time just being part of the team versus the leader of the team. I was just a lay person now. I was used to having authority.

It was a relief in the beginning, but I soon felt held back. I missed the process of picking out songs and leading them. I would lead only four songs a month. I reminded myself that I needed to be obedient and submissive. That was the current season of ministry for me. I did not want to take someone else's ministry because I missed mine. The fact was that they made a place for me when they had all the help they needed. I appreciate that.

December 29, 2013 (Facebook)

"I was supposed to join the worship team at New Beginnings Church this morning, and I just couldn't do it. I am so broken right now. How do I minister to others when I need God to minister to me? I've lost my husband of 20 years, lost my church of over 20 years, lost my music ministry, and had to give up a job teaching that I loved so much. I'm thankful to have 3 students starting so far in January, but it's not

enough to cover bills. I'm living with my parents after 20 years of independence. 2013 has been the worst year of my life. I need hope. Without Jesus, I would die."

I struggled as a parishioner in my new church as well. It didn't feel like "home." That was not their fault. The people were loving and cared about me. A hardness came over me in that I didn't care if I lost anyone else. If someone didn't like me, my opinion was that I had lost the one I loved the most, so who cares about anyone else? I left as soon as church was over and didn't need any new friends. I don't know if they noticed really. I may have been nice on the surface. No matter what, I was wrong. This attitude would last for a few years.

December 31, 2013 (Facebook)

Tomorrow is a new year, I gladly let go of this one. I pray the Lord continues to heal my heart. I plan to take better care of myself. I trust the Lord. I will focus on moving forward. I'm thankful for my children. I'm thankful for my family. I'm thankful that I start teaching again this Friday. I've missed it so much. I'm thankful that I'm a survivor

chapter

3

WRITING, A DEAD RAT, AND STRATEGY

In March of 2014, I agreed to obey the Lord and start journaling. God was speaking into my heart to stand for my husband. The first six months were the most dramatic, traumatic and horrific time of our struggle. The journal I kept covered events of those six months. After that time, my documentation was more on social media than anything. People were following my journey and I had begun ministering to people entering their own seasons of waiting. I opened up more using that medium. Socia media can be used as a diary. Remember when we used to hide our diaries? Times have changed. I told God that if my story helped just one person, I would never hide it.

I have counseled those going through this journey and I have found that the enemy uses the same tactics, even the same lingo. I will be sharing some intimate details because I want people to see the similarities in language and tactics. I also want people to know that no matter how dark things look, God can still change things. I am not sharing these entries from my journal to embarrass my husband, titillate your curiosities, or glory in past shame. There are details that will not be in this book. This is not easy.

Monday, March 10, 2014 (PRIVATE JOURNAL)

"I didn't want to remember... Making a decision to journal again was not an easy one. I've been in a terrible season, so why document it? Because, where the Lord leads- you go. I've already had an opportunity to minister to others through my journey.

I'm turning 40 years old in a few weeks. I'm living with my parents, separated from my husband of 20 years, and starting over. I'm thankful to have our 4 beautiful kids with me. They keep me going. Jesus keeps me breathing.

I miss Cal. The Cal that I thought I knew. The Cal that I know he truly is. I love him desperately. I never dreamed I would be here.

Cal is still living in Ukiah. He has been unfaithful. He has chosen a lifestyle that cost us our church, his reputation, and our marriage. I found out that he was using Meth for a year, which explained the personality change. He has been clean for over a month now, and I pray he stays that way.

He has blamed me. We hardly talk anymore. It's been a painful process. "Process..." What a word. The Lord has been giving me a strategy during this whole ordeal. To what end? I don't know. It's not for me to know. I just need to be faithful, obedient."

When I was writing these words, I had no idea the emotional ups and downs that I was about to go through. He would not stay clean. He would hit bottom, grab a shovel, and dig deeper. I was so sure that this process would take less than a year to come full circle. From separation to reconciliation, it would take almost five years.

March Journal Entry (Continued):

"PROCESS

1. 3 months prayer and fasting. April 20th ends this season. Will I file for divorce or separation? Hmm...
2. Weekly Strategies:

The first thing the Holy Spirit told me to do was: "Don't cry for a week." I had been shedding a lot of tears. Feeling unwanted and unloved are among the most painful feelings in the world. I tried not to cry in front of the kids, but swollen eyes are hard to hide. So, I didn't cry for a week. It gave my heart a rest. I've cried many times since, but it is less and farther between.

The next week's strategy:

"Do not initiate contact (text or call) with Cal for a week."

Calvin talked death so much. I was so afraid he would kill himself. I wanted him to know how much I cared. Contact never seemed to end well for me. He would tell me to move on. He never would be with me again. He blamed me. Hurtful words that I would re-read and let it torture my spirit. I understood why the Holy Spirit would lead me away from this. I felt that I could respond if he contacted me (which he hardly did anyways), especially if it had to do with the kids.

The week went well. He contacted me at the end of the week. We started having positive interaction. I wanted to keep it that way. I decided to stay positive, no matter what he might say to me. This would be tested in weeks to come."

Calvin was his most mean during the first six months of our separation. I would often wonder, "what marriage were you in?" He would say things that just didn't line up with my memories. We behaved lovingly towards each other before we separated. We were still intimate. Who was this man? I felt like a widow whose dead husband's evil doppelganger was torturing me. The journal entry (the first one was the longest because I was going back a few months) went on to talk about the difference a year makes.

(Continued Journal Entry)

"The Big Grace Test

Valentines Day. I was not looking forward to this day. My mind kept going back to Valentine's Day just one year ago.

One year, what a difference. We went to the 101 Café for dinner. It was open mic night. Cal surprised me by learning (that week) and singing "Wanted," by Hunter Hayes.

Then, while the house band played, we danced in the back of the restaurant. Just us. I remember a lady coming up to me saying, 'you are so lucky.'

After dinner, we sat on the lawn of the courthouse. With guitar in hand, I sang "Heaven," by Bryan Adams.

What a beautiful night.

What a beautiful memory."

The journal included the lyrics to both songs.

Music was a huge part of Cal and my relationship. We would often send songs to each other. Music would become a source of torture that the enemy would use to hurt me in the coming years. I don't write "try to hurt me," because he would be successful. I'll share more about that later.

(Continued Journal Entry)

"Wow. Reading those lyrics of his song to me and my song to him- we were in love.

Cal and I texted today. He told me how he can't listen to anything by Bryan Adams anymore. He's told me before how he cries. He's told me before how he'll never be over me. He didn't want "me to leave."

But then... He tells me how we'll never be together again. He doesn't love me as a wife. I should move on. I deserve better. He's in a relationship now .... Yep, he moved on because, 'he would have died if he hadn't.'

I've remained faithful. No papers have been filed. I'm still married. I have not been kissed since before New Years. I miss that. I miss feeling his feet on mine at night and in the morning. I miss so many things. I can't "move on" so easily. I understand why people do. Loneliness..."

Loneliness is a tough thing. You can be in a crowded room and still feel alone. The things that are missing are amplified and can make you angry. The oil in my car needs to be changed. Where is my partner? I've had a long day, and the kids are being disobedient. Where is my partner? "How was your day, honey?" Where is my partner?

Many want to fill that void with a new partner. I had offers. The first man to ask me out was a married man. He would not be the last married man to write to me privately. I remember a man coming up to me in the grocery store and showed me how to pick out a melon. He was so flirtatious and then the wife came down the aisle! She was so angry. I was so offended. I was not offended at the woman. I wasn't even mad at the man. I was offended that the enemy was using this tactic to put salt in my wound, while hurting another couple.

I was still married. I didn't want another man! It was weird to me when men would ask me out. I did not want their comfort. I wanted my husband. I wanted the man who I was in love with. I wanted the only man that I had ever been intimate with. I wanted true love. I wanted Calvin.

My first Valentine's Day without my husband was rough. I joined a gym and that became a big part of my life. I was not looking to have a "revenge body." I hate that term so much! I just wanted to feel better.

(Continued Journal Entry)

"...Valentines Day, 2014. I didn't want to do anything. Mom, Ramona, and I joined a gym and that's the only place I wanted to go. We went and had a great workout.

I received a text from Cal that he never wanted me to leave. He was sorry, would always love me. Then, he told me that he had just seen [the movie] "Safe Haven." I, once again, reminded him that I loved him."

It is important to remember that you have the right to tell someone that you love them. I did not care that he had a girlfriend. I was his wife. I had the rights, not her. Never forget who you are. My dad taught me, "you can't make others do right, but you can do right." Loving Cal was right. Telling him was right. Reminding him was right.

It amazed me how he would tell me he missed me in one text, and in the next text he would tell me that he was on a date, or how we would never be together again. The timing always blew my mind. I remember going to the piano to lead worship at a youth rally, and I received a text about his new relationship. Why would I take my phone to the piano? Because I craved hearing from him. The text notification that sounded like a whistle became something that I wanted to hear, to something that I dreaded to hear.

I was in the DMV a few weeks ago and I heard that whistle notification in the building. I hadn't heard it in years, and it jarred me. It didn't hurt me to hear it, but I had a flashback of when it did.

I don't believe the timing thing was coincidental. Just as God was giving me strategy in this fight, I believe that Cal's actions were being influenced by the one who truly hated me. Ephesians 6:12 (KJV) says, "For we wrestle not against flesh and blood, but against principalities, against powers, against the rulers of the darkness of this world, against spiritual wickedness in high places." I needed to remember who the real enemy was. The timing of some of these events showed the devil's hand. I had to learn to use it as ammunition against the wiles of the devil. Prayer was a weapon. Recognizing his plots through discernment was a gift of God.

(Continued Journal Entry)

"Cal has had a change in his belief system. He is a Universalist now. Everyone makes heaven, so do what you want here on earth. What he has wanted is drugs, alcohol, cigarettes, and women. His selfishness has cost him everything; his family, his ministry, friend, health ...He's homeless and jobless.

He says that he's clean now. I expect that to start bringing clarity. He told me today that he's tired of smoking. He's looking for work because he wants to send me money.

I believe that as long as he believes in no sin, he will continue in his vices. I believe he is deceived by a lying demon that hates him and really hates me. I believe it tries to torture me through Cal."

Sin is real. Grace is real. Does grace give us a license to sin? No. Romans 6:1-2 (NIV) "What shall we say, then? Shall we go on sinning so that grace may increase? By no means!" Sin destroys. Sin corrupts. Sin hurts. Sin has no good qualities.

Galatians 5:19-21 (NLT)- "When you follow the desires of your sinful nature, the results are very clear: sexual immorality, impurity, lustful pleasures, idolatry, sorcery, hostility, quarreling, jealousy, outbursts of anger, selfish ambition, dissension, division, envy, drunkenness, wild parties, and other sins like these. Let me tell you again, as I have before, that anyone living that sort of life will not inherit the Kingdom of God."

I would rather be known by other fruits.

Galatians 5:22-25 (NLT)- "But the Holy Spirit produces this kind of fruit in our lives: love, joy, peace, patience, kindness, goodness, faithfulness, gentleness, and self-control. There is no law against these things! Those who belong to Christ Jesus have nailed the passions and desires of their sinful nature to his cross and crucified them there. Since we are living by the Spirit, let us follow the Spirit's leading in every part of our lives."

(Continued Journal Entry)

"Don [my brother and pastor] **told a story in his sermon at the rally. He talked about a pilot in a small plane who didn't know a giant rat had climbed into the plane. It got behind the flight panel. He was in the air when he realized it. He knew if the rat chewed through the wires, the plane could crash. So, he took the plane higher and higher, elevation rising and oxygen depleting. Finally, due to lack of oxygen, the rat fell out, dead.**

I knew then that I need to go higher in Christ and kill that rat that is trying to crash my plane.

No more would I let it affect me. Cal and I are not friends on Facebook anymore. So, I don't see things anymore. I've increased my fast and prayer life, and I strive for faith, faith, faith.

I want to show love and grace to Cal no matter what he may say. His words cannot torment me anymore. I know their source. That rat demon showed his hand and I'm fighting with him with the Word and faith.

Go to church. The Lord gives sermons to your pastor for you.

(Final section from the first entry)

"Things the Lord showed me:

1. If Cal has been lied to about God, know he's been lied to about me. I am a good wife and mom. We really were in love. I didn't drive him away.
2. I love Cal more now through AGAPE love. It's supernatural. It lets me see past the hurt and betrayal and leaves only pure love from the Father.
3. (counsel from dad) I am stirring up devils! Things seemed to get worse, and I felt like my prayer in the week and fasting on Saturday wasn't working. No, it's the opposite. The enemy is fighting and wants me to give up.
4. God gave me to Cal over 20 years ago. Cal is worth fighting for. He deserves his family.
5. I'm not focusing on praying for "us" right now but focused on Calvin being free. Cal believes that he is free, but he is bound. If he is not free, "us" will never work.

I asked God to use any means to show him the Truth, except one thing. Actually, two things: 1. Keep him from disease 2. Keep him alive.

Weekly Strategies Continued:

The last strategy that I felt has been ongoing for over a month now. I've seen more results during this phase than any other.

Extreme Fasting

I felt that I was to fast til 5pm every day, privately. If someone invited me out, I would eat for sake of privacy of the fast.

Since I was going to the gym a lot, I stopped eating after 7pm. I realized that I was not eating from 7pm 'til 5pm the following day. .It is also to be part of my fasting time.

I fast 22 hours a day for my husband.

Results:

1. I had just completed a month when Cal told me he had a month free of meth. Coincidence? <u>No.</u>
2. My heart is healing. I can listen to music. This morning, I listened to "Heaven" on the radio. No tears.
3. My love for Cal is truly unconditional. Whether we are united in marriage again or not, this will not change.
4. My music teaching business is growing. My bills have been paid every month.
5. Cal has been more friendly. His shocking proclamations have stopped.
6. I have had opportunities to minister to women going through similar circumstances. I have found out that people are watching me and have been encouraged by my walk.
7. I am at peace. I still experience sadness at times and tears still come. <u>BUT</u> I continue to hope. I continue to move forward. I put my hope in Christ. God is working. God is moving. I believe. I believe. I believe.

I'm listening daily. I'm believing daily. Moments of defeat are literally <u>moments</u>. I get up ready to fight harder.

I am a fighter.
I am more than a conqueror.
I am not giving up.
I miss my husband, but I am <u>not</u> alone.

chapter

4

Armor, a Fleece, and Exercise

I am a book reader. I love to read Christian Westerns, set in the 1800's. I have read a few books set in modern times, but I am already familiar with modern times. Going back in time is an escape for me.

I wanted to try a self-help book earlier in my journey. The one I looked at had a quiz in it that would tell you how much help you needed. I took the quiz, tallied up the score and the result read, "Get help now!" I did not read the book, nor did I get help from anyone in the psychology department. I am not against therapy. The Bible talks a lot about getting good advice. We need it. I had prayer partners, but I was not in counseling. I received great advice from my father and sermons at church. I prayed a lot.

I have never been a devotional book reader. But the Lord spoke to my heart to read one every week for a month. When I write "one," I mean "one." It really blessed me and fed me.

March 11, 2014 (Private Journal)

"I just downloaded a new devotional book into my kindle. The first chapter was so good. "The 7-Day Prayer Warrior

<u>Experience</u>"- by Stormie Omartian New assignment- Read this every week 'til April 20th. The first chapter was about putting on the <u>WHOLE</u> armor. We are in a spiritual fight, and we need to be prepared.

Ephesians 6:14-18 (NKJV)

Stand therefore, having girded your waist with truth, having put on the breastplate of righteousness, and having shod your feet with the preparation of the gospel of peace; above all, taking the shield of faith with which you will be able to quench all the fiery darts of the wicked one. And take the helmet of salvation, and the sword of the Spirit, which is the word of God, praying always with all prayer and supplication in the Spirit, being watchful to this end with all perseverance and supplication for all the saints."

Do you have anything that you wear that you do not take off? I have a bracelet that I wear all the time. I love it. It does not protect me from anything. It's a Chain bracelet with a heart. Cal had given it to me on Valentine's Day years ago. I took off my wedding band, and my wedding picture off the wall at one point, but I wore the bracelet as a reminder of my stand. It was a reminder, but it had no power.

The armor of God is something that you wear all the time, and it has power. It pertains to every believer. I love jewelry, but you may not. That is your preference. The armor of God is not about style. It's about need. You need this armor.

Truth. We live in a world where people believe in "their truth." If you say the sky is green, then we must accept that as your truth. If your truth says that you are a turtle, then I must accept how slow you walk. The truth does not change because your opinion about it is contrary. Jesus said that He is the Way, the Truth and the Life. We need wisdom to discern the truth from the lies of the devil.

Righteousness. The breastplate covers your heart. Doing things that please God protects your heart. It leads you to a moral lifestyle. Righteousness protects your reputation. Righteousness makes you trustworthy. I do not want to pick and choose when to live righteously. I want it to be a continuous thing.

Preparation of the gospel of peace. I love peace. I have a "rule of peace" in my home. I do not let things in my house that threaten my peace. I protect the peace in my house. We still have disagreements, but it must happen with self control intact and resolution. If that can't be done, then go take a walk 'til it can. I hate drama. If you can't be peaceful on social media, then take a break from it.

One of my pet peeves is seeing Christians argue on social media. The world needs peace. As my mama always says, "get glad in the same pants you got mad in!"

Faith. I believe in Jesus. I believe in what He says He will do. The enemy seeks to kill, steal and destroy your faith. Satan hates your faith. Don't stop believing that God sees you, loves you, and knows how to get you through any circumstance.

Salvation: I am so glad to be saved. The helmet of Salvation is very important to your armor. The mind is such a powerful place. It's always with you! Bathe your mind in the things of God. There's an old song that says, "I'm saved, and I know that I am." Do you know that you know?

Sword of the Spirit. The Word of God is a lifeline. There is nothing new under the sun. Society is not the worst that it ever was. Religious persecution is not the worst it ever was. Disease, famine, and pestilence did not originate in our generation. The Bible from beginning to end shares a history of God being there through it all. It shows us how to survive from day to day. It shows us life before Christ and life after. For every situation that you face, there is a word for you.

Psalm 119:11 (NLT)- "I have hidden your word in my heart, that I might not sin against you."

The rest of the "7-Day Prayer Warrior Experience" really blessed me. I should read it again.

A Fleece:

(Continued March 11 Journal Entry)

Testimony: "A couple of days ago, I asked God for a small sign. I was wondering if Cal missed me at all. Just wondering.

I prayed for a sign if he did. A few minutes later, I got a text from Cal. It didn't say anything special, just a text. I thought, "is that the sign?" I wasn't sure, but I wanted to accept it as one. Then, God confirmed it in an amazing way.

I went on Facebook and a picture that someone "liked" appeared on my wall. It said, "A text from me means I miss you." I tried to go to her page today to make sure I had the exact words, but it doesn't show on her wall because it was a liked post and not a shared post. God wanted me to get that message at that exact time to confirm the sign. Just knowing that I am thought of and missed brought peace to my heart in that moment. Thank you, Jesus!

Judges 6:37 (NIV)- "I will place a wool fleece on the threshing floor. If there is dew only on the fleece and all the ground is dry, then I will know that you will save Israel by my hand, as you said."

I still believe that God let that happen for me. Even if I am wrong, it gave me peace in that moment and I'm thankful for it. I didn't want to ask for a sign every five minutes, so I focused on faith and not needing to see with my eyes. The Holy Spirit will lead you in when to lay a fleece.

(Continued March 11 Journal Entry)

Exercise

Ramona, mom and I have joined a gym. I love it. This is the first time I've been more focused on exercise than diet. I'm doing this for me. During the first "trimester" of this labor period, I have eaten my way through it. I gained almost 20 pounds. No more.

I also thought of Esther who prepared herself for the King. If Cal and I reconcile, I want to present myself to him as a healthier, happier woman.

Queen Esther prepared herself physically for a year. Start somewhere. I didn't want my weight loss to be about Calvin. It was partly about him, but not fully. The Lord had spoken into my heart that I needed to focus on three things during this journey:

1. Health of Spirit
2. Health of Mind
3. Health of Body

The health of Spirit was staying in prayer and the Word. I held on to faith. Sometimes it felt like I only had a scrap of faith left concerning my husband. I held on to it as tightly as I could. I was in a spiritual battle. I've seen people go through trials and seem to run far away from God instead of running to Him. I needed wisdom. I needed discernment. I needed grace. I needed every fruit of the spirit available to me.

The health of mind was about guarding my thoughts. I had to work on not allowing "stinkin' thinkin'" to permeate my mind. If a bad thought comes in, then get it out as quickly as possible. Do not nurse self-deprecating thoughts about yourself.

The health of body was about taking care of myself physically. I did not want to eat through my feelings. I love to bake. I baked when I was sad. I saw it as therapeutic at the time. I'm sure it was to an extent. I now bake out of love and not depression. The food tastes better. My family no longer asks, "is something wrong?" when they come into the kitchen and find a plate of brownies. Weight loss is also good for your blood pressure. Mine was too high.

chapter

5

New Pastors, Dreams, Wishes, and a Wicked Tango

I prayed for Calvary Way to have great new pastors. They deserved it. When you love something, or someone, you wish the best for them. I wanted that for Calvary Way. When they got it, it was bittersweet to witness.

March 13, 2014 (Journal Entry)

Well, it's been a rough day. Not a bad day, just rough. Bittersweet. The new pastors of Calvary Way have arrived. He posted pics of the remodeled parsonage and the church sign where his name now rests. I remember loving seeing Cal's name there.

The folks met them when they arrived to tour the home, help them unload, and filled the kitchen with groceries. I am honestly happy for the pastors [omitted names for privacy]. They are good folks and I believe God is restoring CWC. But

27

it hit me so hard as a reminder of all I've lost. I looked at the pictures and wept. I've lost so much. God is restoring things in my life, and for that I'm thankful.

I loved my church. They were "my people." I have some precious sisters that still attend there, and we still refer to each other this way. We'll see each other at a conference and say, "my people!" I love that and I pray it never changes.

The church that I have been attending for almost ten years is my church. I feel that now. It feels like home, but it took a while to reach that place. Healing does that. New Beginnings Christian Church is a blessed place. I like to hang out with them now. I don't run away like I used to do.

(Continued Journal Entry)

"I received a private message from a friend who dreamed that she was looking at pictures of Cal and I together."

From another sweet sister:

"As I was praying this morning, this is the word the Lord told me to let you know. - 'You are a valuable and important woman of God. You walk in My favor. Nothing is too hard for Me. I am with you, my daughter. You walk in purpose and destiny, and nothing or no one can take that away.'"

These types of messages always came at the right time. I might be struggling with doubt at the time, and then a sweet message would arrive. I remember once receiving a message from a friend that lifted me up when I was in the depths. She told me how she never writes about dreams and stuff like that, but when she woke up that morning, she knew she had to tell me. This is a woman that I trust, and I know she doesn't throw things out there just to make you feel better. She dreamed that she saw Calvin standing in front of a crowded church, and he was preaching the truth. What resonated with me the most was that he was preaching "the Truth." My faith was lifted that day.

A positive word can go a long way for a person who is in waiting. Faith spoken from a friend is valuable. Support is helpful for tired arms.

Exodus 17:12 (GNT)- "When Moses' arms grew tired, Aaron and Hur brought a stone for him to sit on, while they stood beside him and held up his arms, holding them steady until the sun went down."

I needed an "Aaron" and a "Hur" in my life. God gave that to me.

There were people who checked on me often and prayed for me. There were those who had restored marriages and hearing their stories encouraged me. I wanted their voices to be louder than the naysayers.

God used two obedient pastor's wives to bring me a gift that brought about a miracle. I had been suffering at night. I shared a bedroom with my daughters and when they would go to sleep, my thoughts invaded my peace. I would close my eyes and images of my husband with his mistress would haunt me. It was torture. I would see them in the worst ways. One day, the two pastors' wives visited me. They had with them a giant stuffed teddy bear. God had spoken to them to pray over it and to give it to me to sleep with. I did. God delivered me of the horrific thoughts that tormented my rest.

Be obedient to the Holy Spirit's prompting, even if it sounds weird. I was at a coffee shop one day and the Lord spoke into my heart to give the girl at the window a small tube of lotion that I had from Israel. I didn't want to because it seemed so awkward to say, "here's some lotion for you." I was obedient and she told me how her father would always bring her lotion from his trips to Israel. She had been estranged from him. I was able to encourage her. Be obedient. It can change someone's life.

March 14, 2014 (Journal Entry)

"Wishes

I have lots of wishes. Lots... Apart from Christ, Cal and I have no life together. Christ has to be the head. We couldn't make it the way he believes now.

I wish for:

- Faithful husband
- Sober husband
- Clean husband
- Present husband
- Overcoming Christian Husband
- Truthful husband
- Husband with sound, Bible-based doctrine
- Loving husband
- Non-cussing husband

But I would let all my personal wishes go. All that matters is His relationship with Jesus. My personal wishes ... I must be willing to let them go. If Cal came to believe the truth of who Christ really is, and even who Cal really is, everything else could fall into place."

I was asked a few days ago how I was able to trust again. God healed me, that's how. It is more than the fact that Cal is still in an accountability group, and his old habits have changed. He is so transparent now. It's been an incredible miracle to witness. I can talk about any details from our time apart, and I feel no residual pain. It started by letting Cal be restored. I wrote about it in my journal. Reading it now, I see where God laid the foundation for my healing.

(Continued Journal Entry)

"A while ago, I felt the Lord tell me that if Cal was restored, I would have to let him be restored. I can't hold the past over him after restoration. We would have to start over, rebuild. TRUST AGAIN.

He would be so offended at what I'm writing right now. He believes his doctrine is right. He believes the church is at fault. Even what has happened to us is blamed on the church and me.

Cal is not the man I thought I knew. I know who he really is though. With deliverance, love, forgiveness, and complete restoration, we could start again. We could have a stronger marriage and ministry.

Cal is lost to the Laodicean church right now. If he saw the truth of that and what the fruit of it has been, maybe our ministry could be to save others from that movement.

I wish ..."

Our churches should be a beacon of Truth, hope and love to a lost world. The Laodicean church looks the same on the inside as the wicked world outside. The Church needs to be a place for change. The church needs to remain a hospital for those who are sick. The Great Physician needs to be welcomed. We're not looking to just house the sick. We want them to go out dancing, leaping and praising God- healed!

The world demands the modern church to be inclusive. My idea of inclusivity in the church is that all are welcome to come in and hear the life-changing gospel of Christ. Everyone is welcome to come inside and be treated with respect and love. However, we do not change the message of Salvation. The things that God loves; we must be honest about those things. The things that God does not approve of; we also, must be honest in those things.

1 Corinthians 13:1 (NKJV)- "Though I speak with the tongues of men and of angels, but have not love, I have become sounding brass or a clanging cymbal."

Without love, the lost will not hear your words.

March 16, 2014 (Journal Entry)

"It has been a wonderful Lord's Day. Church was getting ready to start this morning when I got a text from Cal. He said he was coming to visit today. I invited him to lunch.

Church was great. Don preached a great sermon on, "Don't just pray for me- PRAISE for me." I will add this to my prayers for Cal. Praise for him.

Cal arrived around 1:30pm and we had a nice lunch. I made Tortellini and Cheddar Bay Biscuits. There was some almost one week old Mississippi Mud Cake left that I knew he would love. He loves week old cake ...

Cal and I decided to take a drive together. We stopped at a gas station, and he bought me a candy bar. We drove to a nice parking lot and just talked. Then we drove around. He bought me a mocha, and we drove around singing.

I really enjoyed my time with him. It was good to hug him again. It was good to get along and be friends.

I'm thankful for pure Agape love. I praise the Lord for a wonderful day."

A day like that was a blessing, but it would often be followed by a huge blow. We would seem to take a step forward, and then three big steps back. It was a bi-polar tango to a song that never seemed to end.

6

DIVORCE TALK, HURT CHILDREN AND A MISTRESS WITH A NAME

March 19, 2014 (private journal)

"Some days I wish I could give up the fight. It would be easier on my heart. But God ..." -my most recent Facebook post

I feel so tired. Cal texted me about filing for divorce soon. This is how our conversation went:

Cal: 'I'm pretty sure I'll be filing soon. It's hard to talk about ... Cause I'm afraid of losing you the peace and power you're walking into today. I was having doubts but it's not enough to keep you penned up waiting. Presuming of course that you were. Hope is a funny feeling. Love hopes all things. So, I love, but love also saves and liberates the captive soul.'

Me: 'I do still have hope of a future with you, divorce or not. That's because I'm still in love with you. You filing won't stop my peace.' The conversation went on a little bit. I don't believe that he doesn't have feelings for me. He can't listen to any of our songs (he would later start giving them to her). He mentioned on Facebook about feelings of anguish (I had to admit to him that I looked at his wall recently. I try not to ...)

My mom wants me to move on so bad. Other people do too. With all that I know about Cal and how he's living, why do I still want a life with him? Why would I want to trust him again? Why would I want to salvage something so broken?

Doesn't Christ want us at our most broken? Doesn't He pursue us when we're running away? Doesn't He love us unconditionally and want to be restored to His beloved? Am I so far off track? How can I be? I am Cal Thompson's wife.

I'm so tired ..."

Revelation 3:20 (KJV)- "Behold, I stand at the door, and knock: if any man hear my voice, and open the door, I will come in to him, and will sup with him, and he with me."

I read this and I see action on His part and action that must be taken on our part. He is not just standing silent at the door. He's knocking. He's making noise. If you are praying for an unsaved loved one, don't be afraid of the noise that may enter their lives. God will make noise to get their attention. Trust God. It's more than just hearing the noise of the knock. The door must be opened willingly. He is a gentleman. He will not barge into a heart where He is not welcomed.

I didn't want to be afraid of divorce. Cal did not file at that point in time. In fact, it would come up many times until he finally filed. My divorce papers came in the mail the day before I left for Israel. That will be an interesting chapter for you to read. A hurt, angry woman on the loose in Jerusalem. The police were called on me once. I'm serious.

(Journal entry continued)

"I had an amazing 2 hours at the gym. The Lord spoke to me so clearly through my sweat and prayers.

'Letting go is not giving up.'

I sent Cal a text telling him this and that I let him go. He can file. It doesn't mean that I give up hope of future reconciliation. I know that Cal and I can't be together as he is. We are unequally yoked. I will keep praying and believing for him. I let go of "us," but I let it go to God.

Take it, Lord. I give Cal to You. I give my hopes to You."

Calvin didn't write me back for a few days. My journal went on to talk about specific issues I was having with my children. I will paraphrase for the sake of their privacy.

My children are wonderful. They were tough, but they were hurting. Hurt will bring about emotional outbursts, behavior issues, and self-esteem issues. These are common issues. We would get into a routine and then Cal would visit. That would often disrupt our flow. I was careful how I spoke about their dad. I wanted to protect their road to reconciliation with him. A bridge on that road would get burned, and I would try to rebuild it as quickly as possible. I didn't want them to hate their father. My words and actions mattered.

My desire for them was to draw closer to God during this trial. It was hard. I shared a bedroom with my daughters, and my boys shared a bedroom. Privacy was an issue. I am thankful for the experience because it brought me closer to my children. It changed my relationship with them for the better. We survived this experience together.

My children would eventually have their relationship restored with their father. I couldn't force it. They each came around when they were ready to. Calvin would miss out on time that can never be returned. A wedding would be missed. The birth of our first grandchild would be missed. Calvin lost so much during his time away. The enemy stole that time.

A Mistress with a Name:

March 23, 2014 (Journal entry)

"I am beyond crushed. A friend notified me that Cal said he's in love on Facebook and tagged her name. (name omitted for privacy) **I know her. I sent her a private message about how I feel ..."**

I must confess here that it was not a kind message. I was blocked on Facebook from that day to present. It would be a struggle that God eventually healed me of. I had violent fantasies of "mopping the floor with her." I had grace for Cal, but none for her. I remember telling Cal to never bring her to my house. I would put her in the hospital. I meant every word. God had to heal me of that, because there was a point where I would have to minister to her. Only God helped me that day.

"I threw my phone and shattered it. I won't be going to Ukiah ever again. I am so hurt. My hope is gone of reconciliation. I feel like giving up. Why have I done all of this praying and fasting? To what end? Why? I love Jesus with all my heart. My faith in Him is strong.

I remember being suspicious of [her].

I taught her kids in junior church. She sat in my congregation week after week. She was married too. My heart broke for her family. I still don't know when and where the affair started. I don't need those details. I know that she was unhappy, and he was unhappy. In their minds, they rescued each other. They were deceived together.

There is something that I know about the spirit of adultery: It is not a matchmaker. It is not looking to find you the "love of your life." Its purpose is to destroy. Then, when it has done maximum damage, it turns on you and moves on. It would eventually turn on them. But that's not my story to tell.

After finding out her name, I broke the rule I had for social media. I posted a very angry message for all to see. I said her name. I don't remember exactly what I wrote because I deleted it soon after. But not soon enough. People were looking her up on Facebook and then began tearing her down to me, thinking that it would make me feel better. It did not. Facts were facts. She was younger, prettier, and thinner than me. She had my husband. Nothing could make me feel better about her.

March 24, 2014 (Journal Entry)

ME: "Why am I still fasting?"

God: "'Cause I'm not done"

Ok. I need to stop asking why and just do as He leads. I feel like quitting, but I want to be obedient. Divorce feels eminent. I see a lot of "feels" in this paragraph. "Lean not on your own understanding (Proverbs 3:5 NIV))." I'm trying, Lord, I'm trying.

When I finally fell asleep, I dreamt all night of [her] and Cal. Awful. I canceled my morning skype session with [student]. I'm too exhausted. I have 2 ½ hours of lessons later today, so I need to rest mentally and physically. I need a new phone too. I can't think about "us" anymore. I haven't closed the door on the idea in the future. But it would take a true miracle. The only way to truly start over may require a divorce. Of course, a divorce may release my heart completely."

I did not want my heart to get hard. Matthew 19:8 (NLT) says, "Jesus replied, 'Moses permitted divorce only as a concession to your hard hearts, but it was not what God had originally intended." God does not like divorce. It was never his intention for the institution of marriage.

I knew that I needed to keep my heart soft. The hard thing about that is the pain that comes with the territory. You feel everything! I did not want synthetic balms to soothe me or numb me. I understand why people turn to vices during times like these.

Sometimes my heart hardening felt like a relief. The result was always the same. I would end up saying or texting something that I would regret. Divorce would look more desirable. I would let anger win. I would listen to lies about me. Lies calling me **"cruel," "dark,"** and that I was to blame **"for people treating him bad."** He would even demand an apology from me.

chapter

7

MY ANGER PHASE AND A GOOD WEEK

"Now I'm in angry phase."

March 26, 2014

I am bi-polar emotionally. We got a letter from the city about the dogs because of a "report-happy" neighbor across the street. I called dog patrol and reported him and explained. Then, I was headed across the street to rip him up when dad's wisdom of, "you'll make it worse" stopped me (He was standing behind me. I can still hear his voice to this day). But I yelled at the old woman on the porch. Then I yelled at Amy (my sister) who was just trying to give advice. I got in the car and left.

I wanted to talk to Cal so bad. This is the kind of stuff he handled, and I needed to feel like he was with me in that moment. I called and he answered. He helped me a lot (although he wants to deal with the guy in a bad way for making me cry). I appreciated him letting me cry and being supportive. He ended the conversation with 'I love you," and I said, "I love you, too.'

Now I feel like doing nothing. That drama tired me out.

The day was about to get worse. I was in a bad place.

I never fight with my mom. My mom is my best friend. I am a "mother hen" to my sister, but we rarely fight either. My family did not like seeing me hurting. They were seeing the worst of me. They supported me, but they did not support Cal. They had a right to their feelings. They were being affected too! At the time, I didn't want to hear it. I received permission from them to share this next part of the journal.

(Journal Entry Continued)

It's amazing how a day can take a nosedive. I was making cookies, feeling better, when mom starts reading my Facebook post about what happened. I mentioned that Cal helped me. Mom muttered, "He's part of the problem," and Amy said, "I was thinking the same thing." I told them to stop and showed my anger. They don't get it.

Days like today I wish I had my own place. Days like this, I feel stuck here. I appreciate being here, but sometimes I want a place to call my own. Being here is a constant reminder of my situation. I wish I had the money for my own place, food, gas, and bills. I feel like I'm putting people out, even though they don't make me feel that way.

But my being here does not give them the right to say anything they want about Cal. Silence is appreciated. They seem to want me to hate him. I don't. It might be easier if I did, but I don't.

I was so blessed. I had a roof over my head. My needs were taken care of. I was safe. My parents never made me feel like a burden. I never felt that I needed to find a place because they wanted their house back.

Explosions of anger were something that I would face during my journey. I remember being at an amusement park, and seeing something that reminded me of myself. There was a water park there. On the edge of the water park was a volcanic structure. There was a gage attached that showed the pressure rising, then it would start to rumble and eventually explode. Water would shoot through the air and then everything went back to normal. The pressure would begin to build again until the next explosion. That is how I felt. Give me a reason to fight and I was ready. I felt like a strong woman of faith one moment, and a ticking time bomb the next.

The things that made me "explode" were often simple things. I remember yelling for not being able to find a shoe. I realized that it was the little things that I felt I should be able to control. When the little things, like a lost shoe, left my control, I got upset easily. I needed patience for the little things.

March 27, 2014

"I'm not a weak woman, but I feel like it sometimes."

March 30, 2014

"The word of the day is "patience." It's a fruit of the spirit for a reason. I need a supernatural dose of it. I kept feeling that word today. That junior church song comes to mind: "In His time, in His time / He makes all things beautiful in His time..." It's not my timetable. I cry out to God for Calvin. My heart grieves at the loss. I believe the love I have for Cal is God-given. Even if no one understands, including me, I have to trust in the stirring He has placed in my heart. I can feel it. So, through it all I need to keep trusting. I really need patience."

I entered the new month asking God to help me to be happy. I was entering month four of our separation and I needed a break. I wanted to focus on good things. I wrote how I felt that I was being released from extreme fasting, but how I wanted to continue. I wanted to focus on my thought life. I wrote down one of my favorite scriptures:

Philippians 4:8 (KJV)- Finally brethren, whatsoever things are true, whatsoever things are honest, whatsoever things are just, whatsoever things are pure, whatsoever things are lovely, whatsoever things are of a good report; If there be any virtue, and if there be any praise, think on these things.

The month started well. I was teaching music. Cal got a job. I was going to the gym faithfully and losing weight. I was turning forty years old at the end of the month. There were lots of good things in store for April.

Our women's conference was coming up, and I was so happy to get away for a few days. I love leading worship at these events. My mom told me that she watched to see If my anointing as a worship leader would be affected. The anointing is so important to me as a worship leader. The Holy Spirit is a better worship leader than me, so I always stay dependent on Him. I appreciate that my mother watches for these things. She loves our District ladies and protects them by what she allows on the platform. That's the sign of a great leader!

My mom encouraged me not to answer my phone. Things always happened with Calvin before big events. I was not going to let the enemy distract me through Cal. That was great advice!

I wrote of one tough moment at the women's conference:

"Pastor's wives are being honored now. It's hard to sit here. Now the assistant pastor's wives and other ministers. Here I sit, leadership to layperson. I'm not even the worship leader. Lord, help me to take a backseat."

The Word really ministered to me that year. Everything was for me. Leading Worship went well. There is healing in worship. I saw ladies from Ukiah, which made me happy. I felt at peace. Callie had a wonderful time as well. It was good for both of us. Cal was on my mind, as always, but it was a restful time. During one of the sermons, I wrote a little prayer:

> "Holy Spirit, please guide my husband. Help him please. Be his Comforter in the process of return. I love him. I love You. Thank You for Your comfort to me."

I am so thankful for the Comforter. The Holy Spirit will guide, convict and comfort. He is a gentleman. He's not mean. Listen to Him. When I felt the most helpless, praying for Cal helped me. I was not helpless at all.

April 8, 2014

"Cal and I had a good talk last night. We talked about one of his last sermons, "I Hope So." Even if there's just a scrap of hope left, it's HOPE!

> - I wonder if he could ever be faithful? - I hope so.
> - I wonder if he'll turn his life around? - I hope so.
> - I wonder … - I hope so."

April 9, 2014

"I woke up in the middle of the night with an urgency to pray for Cal. I did. I'm not going to ask Cal anything. I'm just going to trust God."

April 10, 2014

"I woke up to a text from Cal. He's coming Friday and Saturday. He also sent me a selfie of himself in "bed." It looked like he was sleeping on a floor. Interesting.

I've had a great week. I've hurt less this week. I'm thinking of getting away for two days in May- ALONE. I want to go to the beach, so I'm thinking of going to Fort Bragg for a night. Sounds heavenly."

Fort Bragg was an important place to Cal and me. We often went there for anniversaries. He would eventually move there with his mistress, and I felt that it was another thing stolen from me. I know that God is the restorer of stolen things.

April 11, 2014

"I had a good devotion this morning. I did that first before I checked Facebook. It's easy to lose time on Facebook. I'm believing for a good day.

Cal isn't coming [here] until tomorrow, so I will hit the gym tonight.

Cal is in town somewhere. I have a fear he's here with [her]. He's not answering my texts. I admit, I asked ... He's not answering.

I'm anxious. I've had such a good week, so I hate that I'm feeling that way.

What is wrong with me?"

There was nothing wrong with me. I had a right to feel that way. I found out the answer to my question. It wasn't what I wanted to hear.

April 12, 2014

"Well, last night was rough. I never heard from Cal. He did say he had limited phone ... I should give him the benefit of the doubt. But now I'm anxious about my texts coming through all at once.

I kind of lost it last night. Callie asked me if, "daddy was bringing a girl." Everything from the past couple weeks crashed down on me. I thought of her being in this town with my husband and I felt like I would die. I have been so nice to him. I ask him how he's doing. He never asks me. Does he ever think about me? Ever?

I'm not ready to see him, but it's not about me. He needs to be able to see his kids. I am feeling a lot of stress. I even went to the office to pray. "Lord, calm my spirit and help me today."

Cal just texted me. All he said was that he wants to pick up the kids, get a muffin and activate Lonnie's phone he brought him. He said nothing about my texts from last night. I'm glad, although I wish he said he was alone ... Part of me thinks he is. Ugh ...

I told him the kids are all sleeping. I wish he wasn't here. I thought I was ready to see him, but I'm too anxious.

I have one week left 'til my 3 months is up. What am I to do? I still don't know. Should I file for divorce or legal separation? Should I make him do it? My faith feels shaky, but I'll cling to that little scrap of hope. I don't know what else I can do besides giving up.

A little later in the day:

I just spent some time with Cal. Lots of tears shed by both of us. [She] is here. Her son has a game here. He cried telling me how he'll never love someone like he loved me, but he had to close the door. I asked him how he couldn't feel for me anymore. He had to ... He still can't listen to some songs and doesn't deny the good we had. When he feels things (like being tempted to be with me physically to help me), he doesn't want to tell me because it'll get my hopes up. I told him that it makes me feel better to know if he feels something, than not at all. That hurts more than anything.

We agreed that as we are now, we are not compatible as a couple. I know this. He is going to file for divorce. I told him that I struggle being the one to do it, but I'm not afraid of it. He hates hurting me. I assured him that I'm doing well. I just struggle sometimes.

He left for a bit. He'll come back to take the kids bowling. I'm not telling anyone about [her] being here.

I appreciate him finally talking to me. He told me how he's trying to build integrity. He wishes he would have started a long time ago, but he's trying now ... money, relationships ... He admitted to being flirty online with women and doesn't want to be that. Lucky for [her] ...Ugh.

Well, I actually feel better that we talked seriously. It was hard but needed. He saw Callie and Lonnie before he left. He needed to get away for a bit. I need to breathe.

I'm gonna go to the gym tonight. I need to sweat.

He never read my texts. I told him not to. I regret them.

It's hard to love someone sometimes.

He did mention "if" we got back together ... I don't know if he caught it, but I heard it. The conversation is usually "never."

He still uses a lot of profanity. He feels my doctrine is so far off. He believes in his new doctrine. God accepts everything. He believes it so much, he's willing to lose everything for it.

The new job isn't producing much money. He doesn't have much. I'm experiencing blessings and favor galore! Does he see that? Self-indulgence has blinded him. "God, please open his eyes."

I am following the true God. The fruits of it show. I will continue forward. I will not fear the future. All things will work together for my good, for my children's good. He hears me.

Cal had invited me to go bowling with him and the kids. I told myself that I needed to be content with friendship. I was going to praise the Lord whether the divorce went through or not. Focus was easier some days than others. That day the Lord also gave me a new strategy:

New Strategy:

Pray for God to reveal Truth in Cal's DREAMS EVERY NIGHT!

I used to ask God that Cal dreams about me. Not anymore. I want clear visions and dreams direct from the Holy Spirit to Cal while he sleeps. Love and Truth."

I asked a few people to join me in this prayer.

8

ONE STEP FORWARD AND THREE STEPS BACK

Over a week went by. It was Easter and the final day of my ninety days of prayer and fasting. Calvin and I were not communicating well. It didn't matter how nice I was. He was doing what he wanted, which was not being nice. He was rude when we texted. He was writing terrible things on Facebook (according to people watching his page.) I had to tell people to stop telling me things about Cal. It hurt too much.

My heart began to harden.

April 22, 2014

"Something is changing in me. Cal isn't communicating with me, and my heart is getting harder. Maybe this is what I need to get through the rest of this season. But is there a risk of not getting it back? That softness of heart?

I'm tired of rejection and hurt. It always comes back to giving him completely to God. I seem to forget ...

I actually feel sorry for [her]. She's not getting the best of Cal. Unsaved Thompson boys are [not nice]."

I turned forty years old the next day. I had a wonderful day, even without hearing from Cal. It had bittersweet moments, but overall it was a great day.

April 23, 2014

"Well, it's 9:32pm and I still haven't heard from Cal. 22 years together, 4 kids ... I deserve a stinkin' happy birthday!

I got a nice text from mom-in-law De. I love her. She knows how much I love her son.

I've had a good day. If I was still in Ukiah, CWC would have given me a big party. I'm missing out on that. But that's the season I'm in. BUT, where I'm missing out on things, God is restoring and blessing things.

April 24, 2014

Callie cried last night. She asked if her dad drinks. I was honest and said, "yes." She's not happy about daddy doing such things. I told her he loves her and misses her. She said, "How do you know?" Callie told me, "I choose you," when I mentioned further visitation

How do you answer a question like that to a hurt eight-year-old child? How do I know if he loves her? All I could say was that I just know. I needed to focus on my children. They were hurting too. They were missing out too.

I reminded myself that I had been given a word from God that Cal would be restored to God and then me. It was a promise. My faith started to build again. My heart began to soften again. I told him that I would do better about sending updates about the kids. I told him that he did not have to respond.

It did not take long for that faith to be tested. The roller coaster is real. One day up and the next day spiraling downward. Eventually things leveled out some, but not in the first six months. I was on a wild ride.

April 27, 2014

"I'm a mess. Today is the 22nd anniversary of our first date. Cal sent me a text at church that he's filing tomorrow. I'm trying not to cry, but it flows out of me.

April 29, 2014

Cal texted me asking if we stayed married, if I would date and be willing to love another? I said no. It's not that he wants an open marriage, he just doesn't care about paperwork. But he'll do it for me since I need it.

He thinks this is all God. God closed the door on us. Well, maybe he's right. We can't be together while Cal is like this. I let him know that this is truly his loss. I know the woman I am. I know the wife I am.

He admits to not being over me, but this is what he wants. It's what he thinks God wants. He's "free." Yeah, right ...

So, I told him to file. I trust God. If it's HIS will for us to be together, it will happen in His timing. Divorce papers or not. It really is Cal's loss!!! It's [her] loss too. She's not getting the best of him. Of course, sounds like they're two peas in a pod right now. Each telling the other they're ok. I still think if I saw her now, I'd whip her!

I shouldn't travel to Ukiah …Jenny, remember who the REAL enemy is …

Those were some real feelings! God would eventually deliver me of my wicked feelings towards his mistress. The way God did it was truly miraculous. The story will be in a future chapter titled, "Praying for Her."

My last post in April consisted of a prayer.

"God, If it's Your will for me to be divorced and to start over, I will. But if it's Your will that Cal and I be reconciled, PLEASE give me the strength to hold on. Please give me the strength to love unconditionally.My heart's desire, first, is that Cal be restored to You- the TRUTH of You. I know You love him. I would even let him go to make it happen. I'm so tired, Father. I'm tired of crying. I'm tired of the dread of a negative text or news. I'm afraid for his life. Sometimes even I see the temptation of ending it all. Some days I just want heaven now. I don't understand this season. But I trust You. That's all I can do these days. Please, bring me peace."

I hate admitting that the thought of suicide even graced my mind. The strongest pull I ever felt towards self-harm happened one day while I was driving. I was alone in the car. I felt the strongest temptation to run my car into a telephone pole. I didn't necessarily want to die; I just wanted to be unconscious in a hospital somewhere. As I felt the pull of the wheel by some unseen force, a picture flashed into my mind's eye; My children. That woke me up! I never faced that temptation again.

Life is worth living. Do not give up hope. If you hear in your ear, "they are better off without me;" Know, that is the voice of the enemy. Choose life. Deuteronomy 30:19 (NIV)- "...I have set before you life and death, blessings and curses. Now choose life, so that you and your children may live."

There were many times that I would hear the sweet small voice of the Lord in my ear. I knew it was God. It would often shake me because I would feel it as much as hear it. My favorite thing that I would hear was, "Do you trust Me? " There was another time when I was standing in the bathroom crying. I looked in the mirror and said out loud, "is he ever coming back?" I heard, clear as a bell, "You have My Word." I knew it wasn't my own thoughts. I was crying out in desperation! I wasn't expecting an answer. He spoke through the noise.

May would come and go. The journal entries would be more of the same. I continued losing weight. My business was growing. Mother's Day was wonderful with my children. The kids and I went to an amusement park for a Christian Music Day arranged by our District Youth Department. I sang there and had a wonderful time. Calvin would be toxic one day, and kind the next. I didn't know that his bi-polar behavior was ramping up in Ukiah until the middle of the month. This would increase greatly over the next couple of years.

The first call about Cal's mental health came on May 15th.

May 15, 2014

"I received a call this morning from [name omitted for privacy]. He was disturbed and wanted to talk to me. Cal came to see him yesterday- no shoes, acting weird. Cal asked for help paying his rent or him and the girl he was living with would be homeless. [He] talked to him very straight. He said he would pay his rent on two conditions.

1. Come to a workday to help work it off.
2. Come to fellowship. Cal couldn't (wouldn't) promise that he would and turned [him] down.

[He] asked Cal if he was using [drugs]. [He] said Cal said, "I asked Jenny if she was Jesus. I asked my brother if he was Jesus."

[He] told Cal he was deceived, and that his kids need him.

I have to trust God. Where is the bottom? I just ask God for protection. I want Cal to live. I want him whole. I want him stable.

Peace, love, SOUND MIND.

"Jesus, I have given Calvin completely to You. I trust Your plan. Guide me in what I'm to do. Let me be a help and not a hindrance. Amen."

May came to an end. On June 3rd, things changed.

June 3, 2014

"Cal broke up with [her]. He's coming to Ramona's [high school] graduation today and looking for work and housing here. I'm fasting 'til he arrives. God is working. I have faith."

He showed up at Ramona's graduation under the influence. I was shocked when I looked across the bleachers and saw him walking towards us. He was so thin! He looked like his brother. He had flowers and a card. He had broken into his mother's house to steal the money to buy them. He was a mess. He kept trying to walk down to the field to give his gifts to Ramona. My brother stopped him from doing so. That would have embarrassed her so much!

When the graduation ceremony ended, I invited him back to the house to celebrate. I let Lonnie ride with him. That was foolish of me. Lonnie said how badly he drove. He was hitting curbs and driving recklessly. When we got to the house, Cal got out a knife to cut the stems of the flowers to fit inside a vase. He started stabbing around his hands and cut himself. Callie was frightened. We all were. I had never seen him like this! It would get worse over time.

June 13, 2014

"He came and went. A few days later he hit bottom.

On Tuesday the 10th, he showed up here. [His friend] took him in. We went to dinner Wednesday night. When dinner finished, he shocked me by giving me a quick kiss on the lips. We had family dinner with him tonight at the apartment [where he was staying].

I'm believing we are on the other side, but still in a precarious place. I'm praying and fasting still. The enemy is mad.

I pray he stays, gets clean, and continues working towards restoration. We are not together, but we are connecting again. Praise God! Callie told me tonight, "Daddy loves you." I asked her how she knows. She said, "I just know."

That was the last thing written in my journal. He would not stay. He would not quit drugs. He would go back to her. I stopped writing in a private journal. I would post on Facebook occasionally, which will be the documentation used for the remainder of this book. There were some major ups and downs to come. The fight would rage on. It would get very dark before the sun would rise again. But the sun would rise again! There would be psych wards, suicide attempts, and jail cells in store for Calvin.

Six months would turn into a year. My belief of restoration within a year did not come to pass. I would settle into a routine of living. I worked, I prayed, I fasted, I got angry, I got happy, I had faith, I prayed for faith, and I didn't give up completely. God was not done with our story. Divorce would happen.

chapter

9

A Song, a Picture and Papers Filed

I expressed my feelings through song writing. I wrote songs with multiple country singers about heartbreak, and it was a great venting tool. You can kill people in country music lyrics. I warned Calvin that there were songs about him being written. Songs with titles like, "Til Death Do You Part, "Don't Call Me Baby Anymore," and "You Don't Deserve a Woman Like Me."

Music feeds the mood that you are in. I've always had to be careful with what I feed to my moods. Why do we listen to songs that we know will make us cry? I even listened to songs that fed my anger. Why? I believe there is comfort in knowing that we are not alone in our feelings. I've heard that misery loves company. Part of guarding our hearts is being aware of the company that we keep. The company of "praise" and "worship" will help pull you out of a pit of depression, fear, anger, and doubt. It's a good time to check your "playlists." What moods are you feeding?

I wrote a song that I never sang publicly until after Calvin and I were restored. It was a prayer to Jesus. I poured my heart out on paper. The venting songs were fun, but this song was the truth about how I really felt. It was the true nourishment that I needed. I had a Savior and Cal was not Him. Cal had a Savior, and I was not Him. You have a Savior.

"You Are"- 06-10-2014

Verse One:
They wonder why I'm waiting here.
They wonder why I have no fear (But I do. Oh yes, I do)
They wonder what I'm waiting for
when all I can see is a closed door in front of me.
Lord, You know it's not easy

CHORUS:

You are the hope inside of me
You are the grace that sets me free
When it all falls apart,
I know who You are
You give me a reason to believe
Beyond all the things that I can see
You're with me, You never leave me

Verse Two:
There are days I wonder if I can survive
and then a day goes by
And I'm alive, I'm still alive
You have proved time and time again
how much You love me and once again
I'm amazed, I'm so amazed

Bridge:
You're with me Lord whenever I fall down
You pick me up and love me off the ground

Jesus has never failed me. People have failed me. Jesus has never stopped loving me. People have stopped loving me. Jesus has never left me. People have left me. I'm so thankful for my faith in Christ. No matter what happened between sunrise and sunset, day in and day out, He was there.

I entered year two determined to be happier. I wanted to be "happy, with sad moments," rather than "sad, with happy moments." Some people like their grief. They like the attention that comes with it. They like the excuses that it gives for their behavior during grief. Some are addicted to their trauma. Healing should be appealing. God would heal me completely. He never left me during the process.

September 16, 2014

Something happened tonight that I've dreaded. I thought it would tear me apart, but it didn't ... I guess I'm stronger than I thought ...

Vague posts can be deadly, especially for a woman in her forties! As soon as I read these words, however, I remembered clearly. I had seen a picture of Cal and his mistress together. I can still see it in my head. They looked happy. I know that a picture can tell a lie as easily as lips can. I have no residual pain now, but back then, pain management was a daily job. I was not drowning in my storm. I was learning and leaning on Jesus daily.

Cal was in Minnesota for a few months. He had family there. I thought he went alone but found out later that she was with him. She left her family, and he left his. He would call me as he traveled back East. He was sleeping in a tent. He was begging for money. He thought about me. She was there the whole time.

September 23, 2014

To fight for something, you must be willing to face rejection every day.

September 24, 2014

"So, take a new grip with your tired hands and strengthen your weak knees."-Hebrews 12:12 (NLT) ... I know you get tired. Don't give up.

October 1, 2014

I almost didn't go to Bible study tonight. I'm so glad I went because the Word was right what I needed today! Please think about that the next time you're too stressed or whatever to go to church. You may be missing out on exactly what would have helped you and fed you.

I love the Word of God. The same God that strengthened David as he stood before Goliath, will strengthen you. The same God that opened Sarah's womb, can heal the barren season that you face. The same Jesus who stretched out His hand to pull sinking Peter from the ocean's depths, can pull you from beneath your waves.

There is so much life in God's Word. If you want to know what God loves- read His Word. If you want to know what God dislikes- read His Word. If you want to see men and women face unthinkable circumstances and come through it victorious- read His Word. If you want hope- read His Word. It's all there! Everything that you need to survive this spinning planet is in His Word.

October 20, 2014

Jesus really said it best: Matthew 26:39 (NIV) "Going a little farther, he fell with his face to the ground and prayed, 'My Father, if it is possible, may this cup be taken from me. Yet not as I will, but as You will."

Our flesh may want one thing, but we must be willing to endure for the will of the Father. He endured for the sake of Salvation for others. Why are you enduring? Hang in there.

October 21, 2014

She is clothed in strength and dignity, and she laughs without fear of the future. - Proverbs 31:25 (NLT)

I would laugh sometimes. Sometimes I would scream. I remember feeling the urge to scream at the top of my lungs while I was driving one day. I did it, and it was glorious! I would sing in the face of the future as well. I would worship Jesus in the face of the future. I would be a lady in the face of the future.

Your mood does not have to match your trial. The fruit of joy can brighten any dark day. The fruit of patience can turn an eternity into a second. You have access to these things as a Christian.

December 3, 2014

When things look impossible, you're in a great position for a miracle. And when that miracle comes, give glory to God.

Excuse me a moment while I stop writing and praise Jesus! I love being on the other side of the trial! I wish that I could go back in time and tell myself how great everything would turn out. The roller coaster ride would eventually stop. The pain would eventually leave every part of my body. My marriage would be greater the second time around! Oh, if I could go back and tell myself these things! I had so much growth during those five years though, and daily walking by faith was a huge part of that. I'm thankful.

January 5, 2015

"Take Your time, Lord." That was my prayer this morning. If getting something done right takes time, then take all the time YOU want! Please give me patience for the process. Oh yeah, it's a fruit of the Spirit! I've got that in my pantry.

January 24, 2015

I miss being in a relationship ... But then I see that couple fighting in Wal-Mart and I think, "I'm alright."

February 5, 2015

I had a great teaching day. I taught 11 students out of town. I got a text during one of my lessons that my husband filed for divorce. That [hurt]... I handled it fine and finished my workday. Now I'm going to relax and watch a movie with my beautiful children. God is good. I'm ok. Appreciate prayers ...

I was rolling with the punches. I was happy, with moments of sadness. My daughters and I went out of town for Valentines Day and played in the snow. Bad news was not allowed to ruin my days. I reminded myself that even Jesus prayed for things multiple times. Matthew 26:44 (KJV) says, "And He left them, and went away again, and prayed the third time, saying the same words." I just kept praying. I was able to move forward without moving on.

March 3, 2015

A positive thing about losing almost everything? You only want to bring back to your plate the things that really matter. I have a healthy plate right now. Thankful.

A few days later, the divorce papers arrived.

chapter

10

DRINK YOUR TURKISH
COFFEE AND BE QUIET!

Those words almost landed me in an Israeli jail, but I'll get to that in a bit ...

March 9, 2015

> Sometimes you have to really say goodbye. God knows how hard I fought. My heart needs a rest. Please pray for me. I'm done. I don't need platitudes ... just prayer for me and my babies. Thanks.

I was scheduled to leave for Israel the very next day. I opened the mailbox to find a package with my name on it. It was proof that my husband filed for divorce. The timing of things always amazed me. Wound, meet salt. I needed to get away.

I was going to Israel for the first time. My mom was going and offered to pay for my sister and me to go too. My brother, sister-in-law, and a church friend were also going. We would have a full day in Paris,

France on the way there. This was the trip of a lifetime. I would deal with the divorce papers when I got home.

I had goals for my time in Israel. I wanted to put my feet in the water where Jesus put His feet. I wanted to pray prayers where Jesus prayed them. I wanted to walk the Via Dolorosa. I wanted to see places that I had only read about.

Paris was nice. We went up into the Eiffel tower. I ate Croque Monsieur in a French restaurant. Delicious treats called my name from every bakery window. Everyone wanted to go to the Love Lock Bridge. Not me. Give me a bolt cutter and let me show how I was really feeling about it. I stood on the bridge and looked at all the locks attached to the bridge. The locks were a profession of love by the folks who placed them there. How many of them were already broken up? I would have preferred to visit the Catacombs and see all the bones of the dead. I needed to get to Israel!

We rented a little apartment in Jerusalem. It was lovely. My mom, sister, and I shared a bedroom. Don and Giovanna had a room, and Matt had a bed in the living room. The living room had pretty windows, and the kitchen had cupboard space with dishes, pans and pots separated for kosher eating. We went to the local marketplace to fill our fridge with fresh food.

Walking distance from the apartment was a coffee shop called "Aroma." I absolutely adored this place! The mochas were so good! They didn't use syrup to make their mochas. They used bars of chocolate. I saw the barista open the chocolate drawer and it's possible that I heard Angels singing for a moment. The barista will hand you your mocha along with a small piece of chocolate that you can either eat or stir into your drink.

We went to the Old City.

March 12, 2015

One of my favorite moments of the day. As we entered the Upper Room, there were a lot of people inside. They left and I was in this beautiful place with my family. Amy and I sang "Amazing Grace." The Presence ... The acoustics ...

Matthew 26:30 (NKJV)- "When they had sung a hymn, they went out to the Mount of Olives." The setting was the Upper Room during the last supper. Jesus had just revealed that one of the Disciples would betray Him, and still they sang. Jesus was about to enter a time of great suffering, and still they sang. I wonder what song they sang? I sang where Jesus sang. What an honor!

March 12, 2015

The garden and the rock where Jesus prayed. I cried like a baby here as I prayed the prayer that Jesus prayed. Oh, that this cup would pass from me, BUT God's will be done.

What a powerful prayer. It was so honest. Jesus was hurting. Matthew 26:38 (NKJV) says that "He said to [Disciples], 'my soul is exceedingly sorrowful, even to death. Stay here and watch with me.'" I know Christians who act like acknowledged pain is weakness. They do not want people to know that anything is wrong in their lives. Are they embarrassed? Do they think that it reflects negatively on God's provision over them? When you do this, you suffer in silence and deny someone the chance to keep watch with you.

Jesus prayed the same prayer three times.

Matthew 26:39 (NKJV)- "He went a little farther and fell on His face, and prayed, saying, 'O My Father, if it is possible, let this cup pass from Me; nevertheless, not as I will, but as You will.'"

When Jesus returned, He found the Disciples sleeping. He asked them to pray again. He went away and prayed a second time:

Matthew 26:42 (NKJV)- "O My Father, if this cup cannot pass away from Me unless I drink it, Your will be done."

When He came back, He found the Disciples sleeping again. People will fail you. He didn't wake them up, but verse 44 (NKJV) says that He "went away again, and prayed the third time, saying the same words."

Don't feel bad for praying the same things over and over again. Desire God's will for your situation. Be honest. I remember thinking, "I know God can, but I don't know if He will." I was always reminding myself to trust in God's will.

March 12, 2015

This is a tough place to be. The place where Jesus was crucified. I felt anger at the attempt to desecrate the place. I felt awe at what was accomplished there, by Jesus. Such a place of mixed emotions.

It was God's will that Jesus would die for our sins. Jesus willingly submitted to God's will. He was a willing sacrifice. What a gift! We went to the empty tomb. He is not there. He is risen indeed!

I loved walking around Jerusalem. We walked on the ramparts surrounding the city. There was a barricade that had been moved, so we ventured into the walls of the city to see the remains of what looked like housing. There was an old cemetery, and there I saw the grave of Joseph Prince. The Western Wall was an emotional place to pray. I placed Calvin's name on a paper within the limestone. I received a marriage proposal. My mother posted about it on social media.

March 13, 2015 (Margaret Cox Post)

Walking in Old Jerusalem and was offered 10 camels for my Jenny. The men here love red hair. They didn't even offer a goat for me. Lol.

I have heard that it was a perfect offer. I did not need ten camels. I already had a donkey at home. The men in Israel either loved me or hated me. The feeling was mutual. I had anger towards men brewing inside of me. It reared its head a few times.

Our last day in Jerusalem would involve going back to the Old City. I wanted to haggle. My brother Don has an amazing ability to get the best prices by haggling with the local merchants. I was successful with my endeavor, but I was snippy with the man when I felt that he was pushing me. He told my mom, "I like her. She scares me."

The second man did not like me. My brother was looking for something specific to buy. A merchant offered him a better deal if Don would come into his shop instead of the competitor next door. The annoyed merchant sat on the ground in front of his shop drinking a small cup of Turkish coffee. He told me that my brother was a "bad man." I fully trusted two men in my life at that time; my father and my brother. Those were fighting words. I argued back that my brother is a very good man. He smugly looked at me and said, "No, your brother is a bad man." We went back and forth a bit until I was done with him. I looked down at him and forcefully said, "Why don't you just drink your Turkish coffee and be quiet!" He immediately called out for the police! Another merchant told my family to get me out of the quarter because they would arrest me. I had disrespected a man. They got me out in time. My brother came out of the shop to find us all missing. He was not happy with me. I was defending him! He was right of course, but I did not feel that way at the time.

We made it home with many great stories to tell. Going to Israel changed my life. We laughed so much. I needed that. The Bible came to life. If you ever get the chance to visit, I highly recommend that you do. Just do not tell anyone to "Drink your Turkish coffee and be quiet!"

chapter

11

FAITH FOCUS, A PRETTY DIVORCE COURT DRESS, AND THE HEART WOMAN

May 10, 2015- Focus on faith. When whispers of doubt creep in, focus on faith. When painful memories surface, focus on faith. Through the good times and the bad times, focus on faith. I believe

May 19, 2015- Something I know for sure: I know how to love unconditionally. It's possible.

May 29, 2015- So many songs have been making me cry! I think about the ones who wrote these songs. There are songs about heartbreak, restoration, blind eyes being opened, salvation and joy in the battle. These are testimonies set to a rhythm and melody. It's a reminder that we are not alone in our seasons. God is with us and there are people who understand our seasons because they've been there. I hope

people see my season and don't pity me. My faith endures. I don't see myself as a strong person. I'm just anchored to the Rock that is higher than I. I'm holding on really tight to it.

I was stronger than I thought I was. I see that now. It takes strength to hold on to something tightly. My feet were planted on the Rock. My priorities were in order. I had paid off our family debts (including the credit cards in my name that paid for outings that my husband and his mistress had taken.) I had lost over forty pounds and was feeling great. I was stronger than I thought.

In June of 2015, I purchased a new car. I was so excited because I did not need a co-signer. My credit score was high. Paying off debts really helped me! I guess that was the good thing about Cal putting everything in my name. I named my new car "George," after George Clooney. Don't judge me.

June 30, 2015-

A lot happening in July: youth camp, 22ⁿᵈ wedding anniversary, divorce court, 5 Seconds of Summer concert, helping a student record an album, and preaching out of town. I will be very focused. God, help me.

Cal did not want me to attend the court hearing. He said that it wouldn't matter. I felt that I needed to be there. I drove to Ukiah the day before the scheduled court date. I met with my mother-in-law for coffee. She was always there for me. She loved her son. I loved her son. We grieved together. We supported each other.

July 23, 2015

It's hard picking out an outfit for divorce court. I had all black picked out lol. Nope. I'm getting out the calm, blue, happy sundress! This is not my fault. I will go in there with my head held high!

July 24, 2015 (multiple posts)

Mendocino County Courthouse

- - I can do this.
- - You can feel the pain, anger and grief in this waiting room ... I'm listening to people talk and it's so sad.
- - That was fast ... sitting in my car ... breathing ...
- - Please pray. It hit me while I'm sitting here in my car. This isn't right. 22 years of marriage ...
- - Sitting in Sacramento traffic, when all I want is to get home to my babies.
- - Home. Thank you so much fall all the love, prayers, and support today. Means so much.
- - is watching "Zookeeper." Love Kevin James.

What a day that was! I'm proud of the way that I handled it. I appreciate the support that I felt that day. I remember speaking to the Judge, and she was kind. I didn't have to sign anything. She said the divorce would go through without a signature from me. I told her that it was "his divorce." There were no assets to split, and the children were with me. No contest.

In August of 2015, Cal moved to Sacramento. He was living with a friend. It wouldn't last long. He was always drawn away. "She" was still in the picture. She would be in the picture for a while longer. Their story would not end well.

September 18, 2015-

I understand how it feels to want to quit. I understand how it feels to have a promise spoken over you, and then time and impatience threatens the faith you're standing on. I understand the midnight hour. Truthfully, I'm past midnight. I've been in the boxing ring awhile now. The count has almost reached 10 a few times. But God ... Get up, He's not done. Even if I'm dripping blood and tears, I'm not alone. [The devil] picked the wrong woman to mess with.

Sometimes my posts would strike a nerve in the Facebook community. I would be reminded by a comment, a remark, or a private message that not everyone supported my stand for my husband. I do not like to argue with people. I dropped people as Facebook friends and even blocked a few. Some people were really mean! One lady told me that she wished that Calvin would kill himself so that I would be free. I DID argue with that one!

September 19, 2015-

A comment on one of my statuses just reminded me that not everyone agrees with my stand. Yes, I know I'm not the only one this has happened to, and I know I have every right to move on. I'm not some lovesick puppy with my head in the sand. Without Christ as the center of my marriage, I don't want it back. For those that don't know, I'm still legally married. The court denied the divorce (who knew they could do that?). Getting out there and "finding someone else" will not make things better. The fact is, I love my husband. I don't want who he is now. I want him restored. I want the man I married. I want him happy, healthy, and whole. If anyone should be fighting for that, it's his WIFE, and that's ME! If you don't agree, that's fine. It's not your fight.

I still do not understand how the divorce did not go through the first time. I just know that things had to be re-done. I stayed out of it. If Cal wanted the divorce, then he would have to figure it out. He did.

I was beginning year three of our separation.

October 3, 2015-

Unconditional love and unconditional acceptance are not the same thing. There are things that I don't accept, but my love is no less ...

I still believe this. I do not have to accept decisions that people make and grant my approval to prove my love. I can love you and not agree with you. I can love you and not be able to be intimate with you. There is a fine line between love and enablement. There were times that I had to say, "no." I still practice this.

October 14, 2015-

The heart woman in me is done. A heart can only bear so much. But the woman of faith in me is convicted to hold on and stand on the promises. The heart woman in me questions every prophecy given to me and my own feelings of what the Lord told me. The woman of faith in me says to be still, know that He is God, and it'll all be worth it. The heart woman in me feels like a fool for believing she could have that testimony of restoration and someone truly loving only her. The woman of faith in me knows the devil is a liar. He uses the greatest thing, which is love, and distorts it to destroy. The heart woman in me is tired and knows she deserves better. The woman of faith in me knows that it's not about only me. There is a bigger picture. The heart woman and the faith woman are both German and redheads. [Goodness], we are stubborn.

There is a battle that rages between the "heart-man" and the "spirit-man." The heart can be a liar. It romanticizes situations and potential outcomes. The movies that we watch, and the music that we listen to will tell our heart how things are "supposed to be." Our friends will tell our heart how things are "supposed to be." Our critics will tell our heart how things are "supposed to be."

I am so glad that I held on to faith. I kept praying. I continued fasting. I did not lose all hope. Hope deferred made my heart sick a few times, but the dream fulfilled would bring the tree of life.

December 28, 2015-

I just talked to the family court. I'm almost divorced. One more step ... Some folks will be happy ... I'm just ready to be done "going through a divorce" and be on the other side ... I don't plan on dating. I'm done with love ...

Oh, heart woman- be quiet.

chapter

12

WHY CAL? HOPE CHEST OF SIN, AND FINALLY DIVORCED

January 9, 2016-

Why Cal? Why was he chosen for me? Did I miss God 24 years ago? I don't regret it. I have 4 beautiful kids from the union. I wonder if he thinks, "why Jenny?" Over half my life ... I hope more people will fight to save their marriages. If God put you together, then why be apart?

Cal was worth fighting for. This was more than just a fight for my marriage. Calvin was sick and in pain. He was walking a dangerous path that would lead to nothing good. I told God that if He had put Cal into my life knowing that I would be the one to fight for his soul years later; I'd do it again. His soul was valuable.

Think about the people that God has brought into your life. You have a responsibility to pray for them. Pray for your spouse. Plead the blood of Jesus over your children and grandchildren. Be a strong shoulder of faith for your friends to lean on. Be reliable in your prayer life.

The world is watching you as well. If you have proclaimed to be a follower of Christ, then you need to accept that your actions are being viewed and judged by a lost world. Don't be offended by that. It should keep you on your spiritual toes! They see that we are not immune to tough times. They may question why your God would allow such a thing to happen to you. Let your testimony share the light of Christ. Let the world see what victory looks like, even while the walls of Jericho still stand.

Speaking of walls:

January 20, 2016-

The court told Cal that if he signed, he was out. He signed. They didn't give him a final date though. He said they would mail me something. Something has happened inside since he signed. I don't feel like a wife anymore. Even separated, the "helpmeet" in me was so strong. The burden for my husband. I feel single for the first time in 24 years. I will never stop praying. I still believe in miracles. But for now, it's the most alone I've ever felt. I am no longer Mrs. Thompson.

A covenant is an agreement. A marriage license is a written covenant recognized by God and man. I have always hated the term, "it's just a piece of paper." Couples have used this saying to justify living together before marriage. I was counseling a couple recently about this very thing. It's called the "bonds of matrimony" for a reason. It protects and strengthens your union.

When you are living as husband and wife without the "bonds of matrimony," there is a risk that you take. It's easier to walk away when the bonding agent is absent. There is accountability and honor attached to a covenant. The marriage bed is sanctified. It is all designed by God to bless your union. Don't settle for a house key over a wedding ring. Marriage is a beautiful thing.

Standing in wait for my husband would become more difficult when he ceased to be my husband. The covenant glue that attached him to me was gone.

January 26, 2016-

True Story: I met a guy once that grieved over his former beliefs. He opened a hope chest that he picked up from an old friend on his honeymoon and inside were remnants of that life. It made him sick. He put them all in garbage bags and threw them away. But he kept the chest. God gave him beautiful things that filled the hope chest over the years. Family pictures, blankets, good things ... A life, a good life ... But, then the old ways, thoughts that formerly filled the chest returned. The same things. History literally seemed to repeat itself from before the chest was emptied that first time. The same vices, the same betrayals, the same heartaches, but with added collateral damage, for he had a family now to suffer in the consequences. I wonder what that chest is filled with now? I pray for this man. Would you pray for this man? You don't have to know his name because there are many out there that fit in this story. There are hurting wives, husbands, children, mothers and fathers out there.

That true story was about Calvin. The hope chest had been a gift from his grandmother and was important to him. We picked it up from a man who had it and brought it to our hotel room. We were on our honeymoon. The contents of the box were remnants of his life before Christ. I remember being more bothered about the letters from a girl than the new age materials.

We threw away everything in the hope chest. Calvin was physically sick. We went out to eat and I watched my new husband process what he had just seen. The hope chest was not the problem. The contents were the problem. The hope chest was created for better things. We were determined to fill it with better things. That hope chest is still with us. It sits in our bedroom.

January 28, 2016-

I just talked to the courthouse. My divorce was final yesterday. It's really official. Why am I crying? This really, really stinks

January 29, 2016-

I will say, it feels nice to wake up and know that I'm not "going through" a divorce. The new chapter has begun. I trust God with what that brings.

I received ninety-five "likes" on that last post. I know that there were people hoping that I would finally move on. One person commented that I was "now living 'HIS LIFE' and not 'his life.'" Now? That comment still bugs me. I never have put Calvin before my relationship with Christ. I was holding on to a promise from Jesus. I was tired of defending myself.

February 15, 2016-

Please, please forgive those who have hurt you. It's not worth what it takes to hold onto it. Don't curse them. Don't speak the language of "they'll never change." They can. Luke 6:28 (NLT)- "Bless those who curse you. Pray for those who hurt you."

I was at a church a few weeks ago and I overheard a phrase that I hate; "Once a cheater, always a cheater." Two ladies were discussing a couple that is currently separated because of infidelity. I was sitting at the same table as these women, and I wanted to argue with them. They know my testimony. Is that how they really feel? Do they think my husband is a ticking time bomb concerning fidelity?

I talked to my mom about it, and she helped me. My husband and I have been remarried for almost five years. The church where I was that night did not know Calvin before our separation. They do not see him as "that guy." My mom comforted me by reminding me how they see the true restoration of Calvin. He is a different man. Those ladies, most likely, did not even think of Calvin when that statement was made.

Think about the words that you speak. You do not know who is listening or what they may be going through. I never want to be the root of doubt that even a delivered ear may latch on to. There is always hope for the restoration of character for any man or woman. I do not believe in "once a cheater, always a cheater." That can be said for any vice! You do not have to be in bondage to anything. There is freedom. There is freedom that endures.

chapter

13

NEW HOME HOPE AND
A PSYCH WARD

Rent prices in California should be a crime. My parents had never made me feel like a burden for living with them. They felt it was a safe place for me and the kids. I agreed. Now that I was divorced, I felt that it was time to get our own place. It would be a new beginning. A family friend is a realtor. I was approached with the prospect of buying, rather than renting. The realtor showed me that it was possible for a single mom to own a home, and the realtor had years of experience to help me.

March 2, 2016

The kids and I are excited! Our amazing realtor has told us to write a wish list. The finance lady will call me Friday and then we start looking at houses!! I never thought this was possible. I have done everything required to start this process and now here we are!! The kids and I are talking about our wishes tonight. Callie wants doors lol. I appreciate your continued prayers for my family. We will be completing this season of transition soon. New chapter for the Thompson Tribe.

This would become an incredibly stressful process. It was not God's will at that time. I can look back now and see it so clearly. Back then, it was devastating. I wanted it so badly! I want to be careful how I share about this experience, because I mean no disrespect to our realtor, who is still my friend. If God says "No," then it does not matter how good you are at your job.

It was a difficult eight months.

March 4, 2016

I want to publicly say how much I appreciate my parents. They have never made us feel like a burden living with them. I can't imagine what I would have done without them. I see why some women feel they have to remarry or even hit the stripper pole to provide for their babies. I'm very thankful for the business that I have built from the ground up and God is blessing it. I paid off all our family debt, restored our credit, bought a new car, and I know the house will come at the right time too. In the meantime, I'm so grateful for the roof over my head and I will never take it for granted. I'm thankful for my kids. I would do anything for them!

I have always been someone that loves looking at floorplans for homes. I love to see it on paper. Walking through potential homes was exciting. The housing market was tough because you had to outbid other potential buyers. The "asking price" was not what you would bid if you wanted to be chosen. I'm a competitive person, but I am also a frugal person. I do not want to spend more if I should not have to.

We found a house. It was cute, but small. The square footage was less than a thousand square feet. There were many red flags to why this house was not for us, but I ignored them. It was a "flip house." There were two bedrooms, a family room addition, a kitchen, and a small living room space. There was a backyard, and a park nearby. The plan was that the girls would each get a bedroom, I would make the family room into a master bedroom, and the garage would be converted into a bedroom for my son.

In the family room, a patch of carpet was missing. I found out that thieves had broke into the house and stole the refrigerator. They used the carpet to pull it out of the house. The realtor for the home said that the refrigerator would not be replaced. We still put in a bid that was higher than the asking price. We were chosen.

The process would be extended due to work that the owners needed to complete before the property could be sold. The work took time but eventually the house was ready for the final appraisal.

The man who did the final check on the house tried to encourage me to pass on the house. He said that the garage flooded when it rained and that he had been to that house multiple times in the past. I remember him saying something about a fresh coat of paint not fixing things. I was too excited and had waited too long to back out.

I was also incredibly stressed. I wanted the process done. I had broken out into a rash that circled my waist. I went to the doctor. It was stress induced. My body took a long time to heal.

God stopped the sale. He spoke into my spirit that "if it was His will, then nothing could stop it. But, if it was not His will, then the smallest thing would stop it." That is exactly what happened.

There was a problem with our bid. The bid was $5,000 higher than what I was approved for. The finance person was working to add to the loan. The company agreed to add my daughter on to the loan, but she had to prove that where she worked required her esthetician license to be an employee. The reason for that was that she was a recent graduate from Paul Mitchell and had not started working in a spa yet. She was working at a professional beauty supply store. If she needed her license to work there, then they could add her schooling to her time in the business.

The finance company said that everything would work out and to sign the final papers. We met at the house, and I signed the papers. The home was to be mine. I received a call the next day that we needed a signature from my daughters' boss stating that she needed her license to be employed. We would get the house if we were willing to do this. The word that the Lord spoke into my heart was so clear. This was the small thing that He had spoken of. I would not buy this house on the foundation of a lie. We let the house go. I am so glad that we did. God had something better in mind.

The months of trying to buy a house were filled with so many ups and downs. The stress on my body and mind was wearing me down. God sustained me through it all. The beginning of those months began with a dream.

March 18, 2016

I had an amazing dream last night. I was standing in front of a mountain. Then, like a scene in one of those disaster movies, I saw a flood start pouring down the mountain. I turned and ran. I looked behind me in time to see the water overtake me. I put my arms out and had the most amazing body surfing experience lol. I had a moment, as I was nearing a city, when I thought "how will it end? Will I crash into a building?" But I didn't. I survived.

It amazes me to read this now and see how the Lord was trying to show me that everything would be okay. It was a prophetic dream about the ride to come, but that I would survive it. I could still put my arms out and ride the waves in confidence. I choked on the water a few times, but I did not drown.

Cal felt worse than I did. He was in bad shape mentally and physically and had decided to check himself into a hospital. I had a trip planned with my daughter and I knew that I needed to go on that trip no matter what was happening with Cal.

March 18, 2016

He made it to San Juan hospital. Thank You, Jesus!! Pray for wisdom for the doctors and that they give Cal what he needs. I'll be in Southern California until Sunday night. This is good though, because it was something that he had to do himself. I'm so proud of him. NOW is the time!!!

March 18, 2016

I wish so much that I knew what is happening with Cal, but I know he is in God's hands. The timing of this is not a mistake. This trip with my daughter has been in the works for 5 months. We will not worry. We will cherish this precious time together. God is in control.

March 19, 2016-

I just talked to Cal. He is in the hospital, and they are taking good care of him. He will be analyzed in a few days and then they decide what happens from there. He's missing me and the kids. Please keep praying!

March 21, 2016-

Update on Cal: He was moved to a new facility last night. He is happy with it because he feels hope there. They want to help him get well now and help with preparing for the future. I will be visiting soon and hopefully talking to the doctor myself. He is thinking about alot of things- his beliefs, his family, his future. It's alot for him to process. Please continue to pray for him. I appreciate all the prayers and love.

The facility was a Psych Ward. It was a place that you did not just walk into to visit. He was behind locked doors. I had to be let in and our visit had to be supervised. They took my purse from me. It was more than I imagined. I remember Cal introducing me to the guard as his wife. Cal gave me his Facebook password and wanted me to clean out his page. I felt hope. When I left the building, I felt overwhelmed.

March 22, 2016-

I visited Cal today. It was emotional to see him in a place like that. I held it together until I left the facility and then

the tears came. Thank you, mama in love Delaine Cooke for talking me through it on the phone while I sat in the parking lot crying. Thank you, mom, for taking me to Leatherbys when I got home. You both know how much I love Cal and want him to make it through this. I couldn't do this without strength from God and the support of my friends and family. Thank you.

Cal would stay in the psych hospital for a little while and then be moved to a transition house. I visited him once and then he left. He was not happy with me for what I did to his Facebook page. I deleted every picture of [her]. I deleted so many people from his friends list. I read his private messages before I deleted them. That was interesting, to say the least.

Calvin would go back to Fort Bragg, and to her.

chapter

14

IDENTITY ACCEPTANCE, MEMORY WALLS, AND TRIGGERS

August 11, 2016-

Going through a divorce stinks. Being divorced stinks. I hate the moniker "ex-wife." BUT!!! And this is a big but! That's NOT my identity!! It's an experience. It's a season. It has affected who I am today, BUT it's not the sole definition of who I am as a woman, nor does it make me less of a woman. I am God's girl. I am strong. I am happy. I am Jenny.

I love being me. I love my life. I am a child of God. That is my identity. I am who He says that I am. I want the adjectives that describe me to line up with the person who He created me to be. I am an overcomer. I am faithful. I am a fighter. I love Jesus with all my heart.

I can be an over-thinker. I miss the mark in this department. I can preach, "Know who you are, and I am awesome," and then turn around and tear myself up in thought. I battle thoughts of the mind often. I know what it is like to argue with the truth. I am so glad that the Lord is patient with me. He will remind us of the truth about who we are. The noise of the world will try and tell you who you should be. Listen to Jesus. He is the Way, the Truth and the Life.

The season that you are in does not define you. Know who you are. Walk in that knowledge with confidence. God knows the finest details of your situation. He sees what we cannot see. Trust Jesus with the details. "Lord, remind me if I forget."

August 14, 2016-

Are you fighting a battle tonight? If all you have is a scrap of faith left- cling to it!! A little hope is better than no hope. Trust in the Lord with ALL your heart and lean NOT on your own understanding.

Deuteronomy 31:8 (NIV)
"The LORD Himself goes before you and will be with you; He will never leave you nor forsake you. Do not be afraid; do not be discouraged."

Let the Word of God remind you of who you are in Him. The Living Word will be there when you are starving for hope, understanding and direction. Psalm 119:11 (KJV) says, "Thy word have I hid in mine heart, that I might not sin against thee." We need to know what pleases God. The Word written on your heart will also be there for you when you need help. The Bible says that I can walk through the Valley of the shadow of death (Psalm 23:4) and He will be with me. I am not to set up camp in that valley! Memories from the Valley floor may surface from time to time, but it is not a sign to return to that valley. Walk out of that Valley and stay out!

Facebook has a function that I call a "memory wall." Every day, you can see your activity during your past years on Facebook. It can be very encouraging, but it can also be like a knife in the gut. It is a reminder of the mountain tops and the valleys that we have experienced. I began posting reminders of where I had been to show how far the Lord had brought me.

I shared the memory of my very first post:
"I am so sorry. Please pray and give me privacy."

September 5, 2016-

Wow, it's hard to believe that it's been 3 years since my whole world changed. I entered the most painful season of my life. I believe that I've become a better mom, a better person, and I've grown closer to God in all of this. God has provided for us financially. I was able to pay off all family debt. I don't know what the future holds, but I know God is there. It's all going to be ok.

Life was moving forward. Calvin was living in Fort Bragg. I took the girls to see him sometimes. He was working various jobs. He was living with [her]. My business was thriving, and I was happy. I had considered dating, but it did not seem right. Yes, I was moving forward, but I did not want to give up.

August 20, 2016-

I understand why people rebound into a new relationship. I do. BUT, if your heart is still with someone else, don't bring that into a new relationship. It's not fair to the other person, just because you want someone to hold your hand. Get a puppy... #singleisok

It is okay to be still and wait on the Lord. It is a wise thing to do.

September 9, 2016-

There are 2 songs that are salt in the wound of my heart. One of them has been requested multiple times by voice students over the last 3 years. It was just recently requested again, and although my heart sank, I did not show it. I will teach that kid to sing it and sing it well! That's professionalism. DON'T bring your personal issues to your workplace. Do your job. Smile.

Triggers. I could be sitting still one moment and then be hit with a trigger that made me want to put on my running shoes next. Music was a trigger. Is there something that steals your calm? That is bondage. The Lord did not want me to be in bondage to a song. If it steals your joy, then it has too much power over you.

September 11, 2016-

It amazes me how some things will trigger grief in me. It can be a good thing that triggers it too. I can be happy for someone's gain and feel complete grief that it came because of my loss. Not jealous, not mad... just grief. But God has been so so good and faithful to me. Rejoice with those who rejoice. Weep with those who weep.

There are people currently going through what I went through. I remember seeing folks get their breakthroughs. I would see couples restored. I wanted my miracle too. I did not want people to stop sharing their triumphs. The testimony is too valuable! Please, do not be angry or jealous when you see people receiving something that you are praying for. Rejoice with them.

Does anything from those five years of battle trigger me today? No. I have been completely healed of all traumas associated with that experience. I can hear [her] name and it does not hurt me. I can talk about the darkest details of that season and feel no pain. I can remember. I am not in bondage to a memory.

chapter

15

WILL YOU MARRY ME? NO.

September 15, 2016-

Cal just proposed to me... Nope. It's definitely not time for that... Ugh... Jesus, help my heart.

September 16, 2016-

I'm not getting married. Some misunderstood my post. Sorry. I know that people know that I've been praying for reconciliation, so this seems like an answer to prayer. But, it's not. There's so much more involved. God knows. I have peace in my heart that God's timing will be perfect. This isn't it...

God's timing is perfect. I believe that it would have been a disaster if I had taken Cal up on his offer at that time. He was having a moment. He was not done with his sin. I believed God when He said that Cal would return to Him first and then to me. Cal may have backed out by the end of the day, but it felt good to be the one to say, "no." Cal was not in control of our restoration story, Jesus was.

I went to a Ladies Conference a month later. I shared a picture on social media of balloons being released into the air on the final day of the conference. I don't remember the sermon that prompted the activity, but I wrote about what it meant to me.

October 12, 2016-

I thought to myself, "why would someone want to go back to someone who cheated on them?" Then I realized that people are probably thinking the same thing about me... Every journey is different. There is healing after infidelity. Trust can be restored. For me, it can only come with unity of faith. Which is why I'm still single lol. I let it go with that prayer request on the balloon Saturday. I've never been more content. I'm in the right place. There are some amazing things coming.

There is hope after infidelity. There is hope after any kind of separation that needs a restoration. True restoration is a powerful and possible thing. Do not give up hope. Don't let the enemy steal your promise. Hold on to peace. Hold on to faith. Remember why you started fighting for restoration in the first place. There will be people who do not understand. That is between them and God.

October 14, 2016-

I've come a long way on this journey. There are still some tough times. Callie was upset about her dad last night. She misses him and wants him well. I do my best to comfort her and we pray together. People have questioned me, sometimes rebuked me over my stand for Cal. But, there are more people affected by this than me. My kids deserve to have a dad. Not a replacement to fill a void, but to have their dad. I don't want a replacement either. I want what I

was promised and the gift I was given back in 1992. I still love the man I knew... I feel like a widow that has to see her dead husbands twin running around. It can be torture... Lazarus, you stink. Wake up!

I was holding on to the promise. I am not judging people who have a different story ending than I have. I am not slapping anyone in the face for the decisions they made. I understand those who move on. Everything for me came down to a promise. I knew that I had a promise from God for restoration.

I visited a church, and someone spoke over my situation. He said that there were two roads that I could take. One would be harder, and one would be easier. Whichever road that I chose, I would be happy. I remember privately laughing about that Word because I did not believe it was prophetic. I felt like it was another instance of someone telling me something to make me feel good and take the pressure off. I would have rather he told me that the difficult road was worth the trip. "Stay on it." God's Will was attached to the difficult path. Was his message to me wrong? Not necessarily. God would have been with me no matter what. I am sure I would have been happy. God had better plans for me.

Those plans included my first grandchild! I love being a grandmother!

October 27, 2016-

Guess who's going to be the greatest grandma on the planet??? ME BABY!!! I can't wait for 2017! I'm so in love already!!!

Yes, the first Christmas gift I bought the other day was for my grandbaby. I have been dying to share!! Finding out that I'm going to be a grandma has changed my life. My baby is having a baby. It's so amazing. My kids are my life. They are my joy. They are my gift from God. And now this grandbaby just makes my heart want to burst. I'm so in love with this little person. I can't wait!!!

Having a grandson would help Cal turn his life around. It gave him another reason to try. He would miss the birth of his grandson.

I was entering year three of my journey. I missed Cal, but I was looking forward to the future. I was tired of the struggle. I was tired of the wait. I had a few moments where I had all but given up completely. I was so close to being done with it all. There is a saying, "it always gets the darkest just before daylight." The turnaround was coming. I did not know how close it was.

December 9, 2016-

Tomorrow I will have been here 3 years. Seems hard to believe. I'm ready for 2017. I'm done with this transition that I still feel I'm in. I'm tired of waiting for a miracle. I'm tired of people prophesying over me that such and such is gonna happen. I'm tired of memes saying that the moment you want to quit is the time your miracle will happen. Please! You know how many times I've wanted to quit, but held on because of fear I would miss my miracle and the pressure of being "strong" and an example of faith??? I'm exhausted of this. I'm tired of crying. I'm tired of grieving over a man who never fully loved me and wants his former mistress, the only true love that he always wanted, who now lives with someone else (she ran off with another man). **It is what it is. I don't even want another man. Why invest in someone who may never really love me either?? Forget that. I've got my kids. Soon I'll have a grandson. Those are miracles and worth every minute of the lie that was my marriage. I love God. I'm not mad at Him. I am blessed. I have almost everything. That's enough til Jesus comes.**

Whew! That was heavy. Cal was pining for [her]. He would beg for people to set up a meeting with her. She was done with him for good. She ran off with someone close to Cal. This person lived with them. Cal would end up living on the streets. He was a drug addict. He was not well.

My Aunt Donna responded to my post written above. She passed away a few years ago. She was an encouragement to me. I want to share her response as a testament to who she is (she's alive in heaven without a doubt). "I miss you, Aunt Donna."

Aunt Donna response:

Jenny, if you can just enjoy today. God brings us special blessings each day. Stings come that stir our flesh and rightly so, but it sends us to our knees to handle it the Holy Spirit's way. Don't worry about a man. When healing comes and you and God are ready, we will see that miracle God brings. Have a wonderful Christmas and yes you are blessed.

It was such an encouraging response. People were praying for me. I was never alone in my dark moments. I would adjust my focus and move forward.

December 10, 2016-

Sometimes I have rough moments. A date, or a picture or something can sometimes take me to a rough place. There are things that I believe to be true, but I'll listen to a lie for a moment. Hope deferred makes the heart sick. I get heart sick at times. I have to focus a little harder some days. I will do that today. Promise.

Have you been listening to lies? Are you heart sick? Focus. I love the rest of the verse about hope being deferred. Proverbs 13:12 (NIV)- "Hope deferred makes the heart sick, but a longing fulfilled is a tree of life." It is so easy to focus on the pain. There is not a period after the word "sick." There is a comma. It is just a pause within the sentence. Do not put a period where God placed a comma. I think my mama said that once.

January 2, 2017-

It takes a day to build a shack. It takes years to build a palace. Have patience and keep building. It's worth it!.

January 5, 2017-

Building a life with someone is WORK! It takes two. Couples can get a little lost in the work dust, but you don't drop the hammer and leave the work site, leaving it to one to build alone or stinking hire another contractor to finish the job. Get help if you need it! Build a life and then enjoy it 'til you're dead... is that so hard???

January 7, 2017-

You can love someone unconditionally and not be able to be with them unconditionally...

A new year had arrived. This new year would bring what I had been waiting for. It would be difficult, but amazing to witness.

chapter

16

PRAYING FOR HER

I needed to forgive the woman that my husband fell in love with. It was vital to my healing. I would not be free until I let her go. I shared a picture on social media that talked about letting the mistress go. I addressed it briefly, but the story of how it happened goes much deeper. The timeline goes back a few months before this post.

January 9, 2017-

The first time I could truly pray for her, I wept. I knew I had forgiven her. Before that day, I struggled with thoughts of violence towards her. I had grace for everyone but her. God healed me...

I fantasized about beating her up. I knew that I could. I remember telling Cal to never bring her to my house. I would put her in the hospital. I meant it. I did not trust myself to see her in person. I had so much anger towards her. I had grace for everyone but her. My husband was her pastor! He should have been more responsible. Yet, I blamed her.

Things had to change.

Before the pandemic of 2020, I traveled four days a week. I taught in different towns throughout the week and from a studio in Citrus Heights. My driving time was my prayer time. I currently travel one day a week and teach from home the rest. My driving time is still a precious time of prayer.

I was driving to the little town of Cool on the day that the Lord changed everything with a prayer. I was praying my usual prayers when the Holy Spirit spoke into my heart to "pray for her." I think I audibly gasped. No! I did not want to pray for her. If I could pray a curse on her, I might would consider it.

I needed to be obedient to the Holy Spirit's prompting. The timing of it was important. I would find that out the next day. I began to pray. As I began to pray for her and her family, something broke in me. I wept for her. I wept for her family. She needed deliverance and forgiveness as much as Cal. She was deceived too. She was not the reason that Cal and I separated. She was another symptom of sin. She was a drug. She was being used by an enemy that hated her.

I felt such freedom when I let her go. I forgave her that day. I let go of the violent fantasies that day. I wish I had done that sooner! She was not the real enemy. She was suffering as well. Her family was torn apart just like mine. Her reputation was tarnished.

The timing of it was so important. I received a text the next day that said, "Pray for Cal." I replied that I do pray for him and asked who the text was from. It was her. I asked her if she wanted to talk to me. She had been wanting to talk to me for awhile.

I could not have taken that phone call two days earlier. It was God's timing. We talked about Cal. She was having a hard time with him. Her daughter was graduating from High School and no one wanted Cal around. He was a mess. They were uncomfortable with him.

While we were talking on the phone, Cal showed up at her door. She did not know what to do. He was in bad shape and needed to sleep it off. I told her to let him in. I did not want him on the street. She told him to go to bed and he went. I asked her not to sleep with him. She told me that she was on her monthly cycle and I told her that that is not what I meant. I did not want her to lay with him. I was trusting her to let him stay under my condition. She said that she would not lay with him.

I was able to pray with her. The Lord softened my heart to counsel her and show her love. The grace was real. The love was real. It amazes me still.

Calvin came to Sacramento shortly after that. I let her know that he arrived safely. She asked me to tell him, "Always." I said "no." I reminded her gently who I was.

The Devil is a thief. The song "Always" was in our wedding. That did not belong to her. The enemy knew that. Remind the devil who you are. Remember who he is. He is a thief and a liar. Do not fall for his tricks to steal your peace and joy.

I remember feeling the offense when her and Cal got back together. I did not communicate with her. I was not in bondage anymore. I was not obligated to her either. Their story would end badly. They bounced back and forth until the final nail was hammered in the coffin.

Luke 6:27-28 (NIV)- "But to you who are listening I say: Love your enemies, do good to those who hate you, bless those who curse you, pray for those who mistreat You."

Proverbs 24:17 (NIV)- "Do not gloat when your enemy falls; when they stumble, do not let your heart rejoice."

Do you need to forgive someone? Start the process by praying for them.

chapter

17

HELLO MIRACLE!!

2017 started like the rest. It would not end the same as previous years. The tree of Life would come into sight for my hope. Cal and I were Facebook friends again. That could always change by days end. He was living in a shelter in Fort Bragg, but he was burning those bridges quickly. He was angry and disruptive. Society was turning its back on him.

January 15, 2017-

This is a prayer request. I've blocked Cal from this post, although we are Facebook friends. I need peace in my heart. Cal will officially be homeless tomorrow and is letting his phone go as well. He can't work. He feels people are inside his head and his personality is extreme highs and lows. He is into a belief system that has demonic activity attached. He sees them and feels them. He talks to the dead...

Sometimes he asks to come home, but it's under his conditions. As much as I love him and I want to protect him, I cannot have that toxicity around me or our children.

I can't enable his addictions. Loving an addict is so hard. He doesn't want to be alone.

He wishes for his ex-mistress, but that's because he really believes that she loved him more than me. He said that she was willing to leave her children, her family, her reputation, her husband, everything for him. That was real love to him. Not to me. It didn't work out.

This is more info than I usually give, but I'm desperate for specific prayers to be prayed. Three of his children have pretty much given up and cut him off, and my baby is struggling with it. She wants her dad but doesn't want me with him because he "scares her." I'm strong, but as a woman, it hurts so much to see the only man I've ever loved tormented, lost and crying out for another.

The core of this is spiritual. He has been deceived. His personality, looks, everything are so so different. I feel like a widow that has to see her dead husbands evil twin running around.

Every time I profess faith that Cal will be healed, and I will keep fighting for him, something major bad happens. The enemy tries so hard to get me to quit, and he's almost succeeded on occasion.

I need you to pray for 6 things:

1. Keep him alive
2. Free of contracting any disease
3. That he sees the Truth and that a flood of grace will be there to comfort him when he realizes the Truth.
4. Full restoration of his mind
5. Bring him home

6. I pray these words from a story sis Trowbridge preached about a woman who prayed her son back from the dead. "Holy Spirit, wake him up. Holy Spirit, make him normal."

All those prayers were answered.

The first place that Cal tried was Victory Outreach in Ukiah, California.

January 31,2017-

Cal is going on [a] 2-week blackout at Victory Outreach program!!! I'm so thankful!! Please pray he stays and that this is the beginning of healing.

February 3, 2017-

It's weird knowing that there's no way to communicate with Cal. In the 3 years we've been apart, we've maybe gone a week without any communication. Callie wanted to talk to her daddy the other night and I had to explain to her what a blackout is and that's it's a good thing. Daddy's in a good place. God, please let this stick... We are ready for a miracle.

It did not stick.

February 4, 2017-

Last I heard, Cal was walking to Jack in the Box in Ukiah. He plans to sleep there if he can't get a ride to Fort Bragg. He's hungry. He's cold. If anyone wants to reach out to him, maybe put a little food in his belly and a kind word, please do.

February 9, 2017-

It hurts when someone you care about drops and blocks you. I've been fasting all week for this person and the situation has gotten worse. And now I'm told I'll never hear from or talk to this person again. Makes me want to break my fast early... but I know better.

February 10, 2017-

I'm getting sick of people saying to me, "maybe he's not meant for you" and things like that. It's usually from people who didn't know Cal before, or well. Or they just want me to move on which is now the "normal" thing to do in this world. So, here is my response to that, that I've already said to two people this week alone.

"You know, I have thoughts like that. But people who know the whole story understand why I keep banging on that door. This is not the story of a couple married for 23 years that just fell out of love, one moved on, and the other doesn't accept it. This was a happy marriage, a strong ministry and a great husband, father and friend. When he lost his true faith, he lost everything. His mind, his health, his reputation, everything. He's forgotten who he was and who we were. A man with an amazing work ethic now has none. His personality changed to someone we hardly recognize. I fight for him not out of selfishness for myself. I fight for him because he's lost, confused and believing a complete lie. It's cost him everything. If anyone should be fighting for him, it's the one who promised for better or worse, richer or poorer, sickness or health. Until God Himself releases me, I'll keep banging on that door."

So PLEASE quit saying things like that to me. I'm not a [silly], head in the proverbial sand woman. I know EXACTLY what I'm dealing with and what I'm in for. I've had a rough week, so please back off unless you have something encouraging to say.

I will always believe that most people mean well. I have said things that I wish I had not said. I often pray for God to lead me in what to say and what not to say. I want God to shut my mouth if it is being used to discourage or sew doubt. People talk too much these days.

February would usher in the change we needed. Calvin would finally get to the place that God wanted him to be. If Calvin could get to Oroville on his own, the Rescue Mission would take him in. He would start as a visitor and then decide to commit to their thirteen-month program. It was a tough program. He had to want it.

He walked all night from Fort Bragg towards his destination. He caught a bus to Chico. He was picked up by a dear friend who took him to the Oroville Rescue Mission. I felt like this was his last chance. I had confidence in the facility and the church where he would be required to attend. The church was affiliated with the Pentecostal Church of God. The pastors and staff knew Cal and loved him.

The leadership was straight with me about the statistics of success. The odds were not in his favor. I did not want to hear that, but I appreciated their honesty. This felt like a matter of life and death. He needed to change. It was time.

February 24, 2017-

I'm overwhelmed with gratitude. Calvin is in Oroville at the mission. God, please let this be the start of complete healing. I've loved this man over half of my life. I'll never give up believing.

March 12, 2017-

Thank you to all who continue to pray for Calvin. He is on day 12 of a 30 day blackout period at a 13 month men's recovery program in Oroville. He is attending a powerful

church and is in very good hands. We've never gone this long without communicating, so I'm feeling it. I miss him. It brings me peace knowing he's in such a good place. I've been told that he already looks better. My hopes are high.

I remember that peace. The irony is that I remember feeling peace when he was in the Psych Ward and when he was arrested and put in jail. It was comforting to know where he was, even if it was in a hard place. As difficult as it was knowing that he was in a hospital, or jail, it was nice knowing he was safe and alive. The peace of Cal being at the Rescue mission was a deeper peace. He was getting the best help.

Calvin was not an easy patient. He still had anger towards the Church. He would storm out of services at times and show his distaste. The leadership never gave up on him. I will be forever grateful for their patience. The Mission program was strict and full of hard work. The Mission ran a catering service and a thrift shop. They fed him well and he began to gain weight. They fed him mentally, physically and spiritually.

April 11, 2017-

I'm so in love.

My grandson was born. My life forever changed. Being a grandmother is amazing. I am so blessed. Things were looking up. Cal was getting help. Our family was growing. My business was thriving. Church life was great. I was happy.

My son Lonnie graduated from High School on June 1, 2017. The mission allowed Cal to attend the ceremony. I picked him up from the Mission and brought him to Sacramento. What a difference from the last graduation he attended! This was a good experience.

June 18, 2017-

Well, we are on our way home. We had a wonderful service at PBFC with Cal. He's looking so much better. We had a great lunch and then beat the heat in a cool theatre watching,

"The Mummy." Happy Father's Day to all you dads, and the mamas pulling double duty. It's a blessed day.

The months went by. The house I was trying to buy was falling through. I was stressed about it, but everything else in my life was going smoothly. Cal was still at the mission. His mind was being restored. His body was getting stronger. His faith was growing. I would watch video feed from his church to try and catch a glimpse of him. He was remembering... I was healing.

September 13, 2017-

How do you know that you've completely forgiven someone who wronged you? You can think about it, talk about it and it no longer angers or saddens you. I love the freedom that forgiveness brings. Bitterness not only hurts you, but it also affects those around you (especially if you talk about it constantly). I was recently asked what the difference is between surviving and thriving. Well, surviving can simply be just waking up every day and breathing. But thriving is moving forward. Thriving is having joy even when surrounded by unjoyful circumstances. I don't want to just survive; I want to thrive!

I am still thriving.

November 20, 2017-

The house fell through. A "no" does not mean a lack of faith or favor. I believe God protects us in the "no." I'm at peace with His will. It's all I wanted. I'm thankful. I know He has better for us in mind.

I was sad, but God had better for us in the near future! Trust God when the answer to your prayer is "no." Be patient when the answer to your prayer is "Wait." God's timing will always be perfect.

September 22, 2017-

Meeting his grandson

That was a wonderful day! God was restoring Cal's relationships with his children. It took time. You cannot force your children to reconcile with a parent, friend, or any other broken relationship. I could not force it. God had to do it. He did.

December 11, 2017-

God is so good. As I was driving to work this morning, I was thinking about the anniversary of this day. I was broken when I arrived here 4 years ago, but I am not broken now. I left my ministry and teaching and came here with nothing. I now serve on the worship team, junior church ministry, and I have a thriving business. I taught 12 private lessons today and I enjoyed every minute of those 6 hours. I came here in a beat-up old trailblazer, and now I drive a new car. My kids and I are closer than we were before. They are the most important people in the world to me. I gained a wonderful daughter-in-law and the most perfect grandbaby. Things are being added and restored. There is more to come. I am thankful.

The longer that Cal was at the Mission, the more freedom he got. We were able to go to a movie together. We were able to build our friendship. He was doing so well. We decided to start dating again. He was nervous. He did not want to hurt me again.

January 6, 2018-

God is restoring things. Cal and I are officially dating. We are taking it slow, building our friendship. Thank you for your continued prayers over my family.

February 2, 2018-

I'm truly happy

March 18, 2018-

I've had such a wonderful weekend. I hate it to end. Cal spent
the weekend with us. Lonnie and him were roommates. My
son Caleb, daughter-in-love Emi and grandbaby Marshall
came for the weekend too. I bought an air mattress for
them in the living room. We had a happy house full.

Calvin and I did not sleep together before we re-married. I was
raised with the belief of "saving sex for the marriage bed." I believe that
God blesses that. My feelings about it did not change because we had
been married before. I think there would be many Christians who would
understand if we had been intimate. It mattered to us to stay pure in this
new relationship. I practice what I preach.

March 24, 2018-

Christians in romantic relationships: God said very specific
things in His Word about how you should behave before
marriage. There are things designed for marriage. There are
blessings that come from it. Don't expect those blessings if
you're not living right as a couple.

A month later, something amazing happened.

April 23, 2018-

Yes, I'll marry you again

Calvin proposed marriage and I said "yes!" It was my birthday.
Cal was finishing his program at the Rescue Mission. He would be
allowed to stay there as long as he needed. The Mission had a graduation

ceremony. He was a success story. I am so thankful for the Oroville Rescue Mission.

I continued looking for a home to rent. Cal and I would not re-marry until we had a place to live. I put my name in at multiple places, but they did not work out.

The folks who lived in the house for rent on the district property said that they would be moving. I immediately contacted the property management to say that I was interested in renting the home. I continued looking in the meantime. I was ready to start a new chapter in my life.

September 21, 2018-

I get asked at least once a week, "when are you getting married?" The answer is: when I get a house. Doors seem to open, I step towards it, and then the door closes. So, that's the answer: There is no set date.

The day finally came! The house on the District Property came available. We were able to move in on December 1, 2018. Calvin and I got married that very day. We live-streamed the ceremony so that people could join us. My brother married us. My family and a couple of close friends were with us in the empty house. There was a small table with roses on it as decoration. It was perfect.

chapter

18

WHERE ARE WE NOW?

I am sitting in my dining room, just a few feet from where Cal and I renewed our marriage vows over five years ago. We are so happy! I am not exaggerating. We rarely argue about anything. He is my best friend, and I am his.

Cal is very transparent. He insisted that I have all his passwords when we remarried. He leaves his phone lying around. Years ago, that just would not happen. He left social media. He meets with a men's group every week. They stay accountable to each other and do Bible Studies. Cal is still doing the work.

I was approved this month to receive my Minister's License with the Pentecostal Church of God. Cal was approved to have his Ordination restored. Everything is being restored to completion. It is a miracle.

I have loved watching Cal's relationship with the Lord grow. When we first re-married, he said that he would never pastor again. He did not want to preach. My brother asked him to preach, and that lit a fire in him. He preaches when needed and it is a Fresh Fire. Cal joined the worship team playing the bass. He also opens our Sunday morning services.

My mother adores Cal now. That is a huge miracle! She will tell you that she knows the transformation is real. Cal is not the same guy he was before. Our marriage is not the same marriage as before.

We welcomed another grandchild. Alma was born in 2018 and we love her so much. Marshall and Alma call us "Oma and Opa," which is German for Grandma and Grandpa.

Calvin works for an ice company. He loves to call me when he is driving. We talk throughout the day. I am still teaching piano and voice lessons and I love it. I travel often leading worship at ladies' conferences across the United States.

I believe Cal and I will pastor again someday. We are not in a hurry to do so. God's timing is perfect. When the time comes, we will be ready.

We have the rest of our lives.

PETITIONER: CALVIN THOMPSON

RESPONDENT: JENNY THOMPSON

PETITION FOR

[X] Dissolution (Divorce) of:	[X] Marriage
[ ] Legal Separation of:	[ ] Marriage
[ ] Nullity of :	[ ] Marriage

Don't be afraid

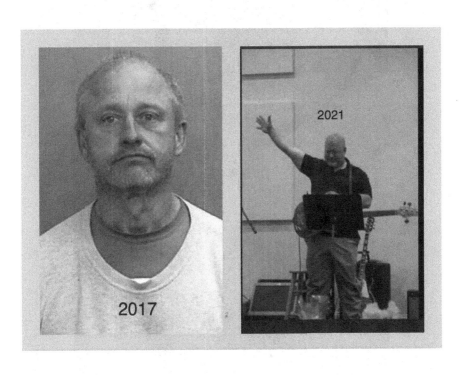

2017

2021

Printed in the United States
by Baker & Taylor Publisher Services